Living Our Story

Living
Our
Story

Narrative Leadership
and Congregational Culture

Larry A. Golemon, Editor

THE
ALBAN
INSTITUTE
Herndon, Virginia
www.alban.org

The Alban Institute
2121 Cooperative Way, Suite 100
Herndon, VA 20171

Scripture quotations, unless otherwise noted, are from the New Revised Standard Version of the Bible, copyright © 1989, Division of Christian Education of the National Council of Churches of Christ in the United States of America, and are used by permission.

The quotation in chapter 4, pages 99–100, is reprinted by permission of the publisher from *In Over Our Heads: The Mental Demands of Modern Life* by Robert Kegan (Cambridge, Mass.: Harvard University Press), p. 355. Copyright © 1994 by the President and Fellows of Harvard College.

Chapter 8, "Living the Story," is reprinted from *Leadership in Congregations*, edited by Richard Bass (Herndon, Va.: The Alban Institute). Copyright © 2007 by the Alban Institute. All rights reserved.

Cover design by Spark Design.

Library of Congress Cataloging-in-Publication Data

Living our story : narrative leadership and congregational culture / Larry A. Golemon, editor.
        p. cm.
    Includes bibliographical references.
    ISBN 978-1-56699-378-4
    1. Narrative theology. 2. Storytelling--Religious aspects--Christianity. 3. Christian leadership. 4. Religious gatherings--Christianity. 5. Christian life. I. Golemon, Larry A.
    BT83.78.F565 2009
    254'.5--dc22
                        2009038220

10   11   12   13   14   VP   5   4   3   2   1

Contents

~

PREFACE
LARRY A. GOLEMON
vii

CHAPTER 1
The Practice of Narrative Leadership in Ministry
LARRY A. GOLEMON
1

CHAPTER 2
The Continuous Thread of Revelation:
Pastoral Memoirs and the Narrative Imagination
G. LEE RAMSEY JR.
43

CHAPTER 3
Pastor as Narrative Leader
N. GRAHAM STANDISH
63

CHAPTER 4
The Sacred Value of Congregational Stories
TIM SHAPIRO
89

CHAPTER 5
Story Sharing and the Practice of Hospitality
as Ingredients in Effective Leadership
CAROL JOHNSTON
111

CHAPTER 6

Have Conversations and Have Faith:
Trading "Us and Them" for "All of Us"
MIKE MATHER
129

CHAPTER 7

Downtown Judaism—in Our Own Image
NILES ELLIOT GOLDSTEIN
141

CHAPTER 8

Living the Story
DIANA BUTLER BASS
151

CONTRIBUTORS
159

Preface

~

Religious leaders across the globe struggle with the post-modern conditions of social life, including religious pluralism, rapid social change, increased individualism, and media-driven culture. How in this panorama of changing practices, conflicting beliefs, and momentary images can we sustain lasting narratives of meaning and value? Given that the master narratives of bygone ages—including religious tradition, the progress of reason, and the utopias of science—have been weakened by this postmodern pastiche, how do religious leaders hope to offer anything more lasting or durable?

Many pastors, lay leaders, and teachers have taught us at the Alban Institute about the shape and power of local narratives. These narratives usually link people to one another, to God and tradition, and to their sense of neighborhood or place. Narrative strategies do not build walls against postmodernity; instead they reframe the momentary images and adrenalized inspirations of postmodern life into sustainable stories. Narratives respond to religious pluralism and individualism by linking individuals' stories to one another, and by finding shared stories—like that of Abraham—between one community of believers (say Christians or Jews) and the next (say Muslims). Effective religious narratives respond to the media absorption of local traditions and customs by grounding people's meaning and decisions in a viable sense of neighborhood and place that is cared for by God.

The essays in this book come from dedicated religious leaders and teachers who use narrative strategies to sustain religious meaning, values, and community in the face of postmodern life. These practitioners of faith—Christian and Jewish—have taught us at Alban a great deal about the promise and shape of narrative leadership in ministry. As part of our Narrative Leadership project, funded by the Luce Foundation, this is the final volume in a series of three dedicated to the findings of the project. In it, pastors, rabbis, lay leaders, and teachers of the faith will find numerous insights and strategies for effective narrative work in their own communities.

In the first chapter, I lay out the context of the Narrative Leadership project and describe the basic intentions or strategies that inform the practice of narrative leaders. Throughout, I share theoretical perspectives and living examples from pastors in the project that show how each of these strategies can be developed. The intentions begin with those of the leaders, who must learn to share their own stories of faith and then move on to helping members of the congregation link their personal stories with the religious tradition and scripture. The next strategies address ways that leaders help the congregation (and perhaps the neighborhood) tell their stories to one another, and how stories from the past—especially "stuck stories"—can be reframed for a more viable future. Then, by engaging their own neighborhood and context with their stories of faith, congregations begin to discern a new story for ministry where they are, and they begin to embody the new story in sustainable religious practices. Most congregations do not exemplify all seven of these strategies, but even if they practice three or perhaps four of them well, they will develop a story-formed and story-telling community that generates new forms of ministry.

In chapter 2, Lee Ramsey, longtime pastor and professor at Memphis Theological Seminary, writes about the importance of pastoral memoirs as a vehicle of revelation. "The pastoral memoir allows us as readers to overhear the sounds of the gospel reverberating through the life of the minister," especially when that story is told with "theological humility," he says. Ramsey explores memoirs by a diverse range of pastoral authors, including Thomas Merton, Frederick Buechner, Barbara Brown Taylor, Richard Lischer, and Heidi Neumark. The pastoral memoir not only models effective ways to use one's own story in ministry, it also invites us to see more deeply how God is being shown and known in the details of day-to-day work in ministry. By learning to hear Gospel in the life of ministry, by living the seasons of the liturgical year more intentionally, by developing practices of justice and mercy, we learn to build a narrative imagination that helps us discern threads of ongoing revelation in our work. We also learn how to find narrative companions—in the flesh and on the written page—who accompany our work.

In the third chapter, Graham Standish, a pastor in western Pennsylvania, shares his reflections on the pastor as a narrative leader. He tells the story of his own circuitous call to his present congregation, its story prior to meeting him, and ways in which the two stories intersect. Then he explores the ways in which humans are "hardwired for narrative" as the basis for meaning making and experiencing the world. He shares a conviction that the best leaders are effective storytellers who help articulate a vision and a set of goals for a community. He shares how effective leaders—like Steve Jobs at Apple—learn to turn around a plotline of decline or chaos into a story of promise. By taking cues from screenwriter Robert McKee, Standish explores how effective ministers help congregations move through periods of crisis and even conflict by helping them transform their inner identity and their outward circumstances. He examines how pastors help churches move through distinct scenes and plotlines of their own stories toward a more promising and responsible story of ministry. Through every worship, every meeting, every act of mission and care, pastors and their church members learn to discern God's movement in the storytelling and creation that is underway.

Mike Mather, pastor of an inner-city parish in Indianapolis, explores in chapter 4 neighborhood strategies of story listening and storytelling that help revitalize local mission and congregational identity. He shares the story of how his congregation embraced a new style of ministry based on discerning the gifts and facilitating the vocations of neighbors in their community. Reframing the neighborhood's identity from a focus on "needs" to one of "gifts" they have to offer was essential to this transition. Mather describes how the congregation began to change its operations by changing the name of the Nominating Committee to Lay Leadership and focusing its mission on gifts discernment. The church also hired a Roving Listener to gather stories of passion and gifts from the markets, hair salons, and barbershops of the community and bring them back to the committee at the church. By using storytelling to bridge the congregation and the community, the church began to link neighbors with other community and congregation members who had the same interests, and to sponsor the expression of these gifts in events for the wider community. By listening to the community's gifts, the church learned to discern God's call to a new ministry altogether.

In the fifth chapter, Carol Johnston, professor at Christian Theological Seminary, shares aspects of story sharing and hospitality that are marks of effective leadership and stewardship in churches. She explores the essential value of storytelling for individual and communal identities. Then she shares highlights of a research project on marks of stewardship in local congregations; in the variety of stories from very different congregations, she discovered that churches with strong stewardship practices celebrated two things: a sense of God's generosity to them and practices of hospitality that reached out to others. She commends a practice of story sharing used in the research to help any congregation encourage the stories of generosity and welcome among their own members. By sharing examples from diverse places—like a Catholic cathedral in San Antonio, another cathedral in Louisville, and an African American Baptist congregation in Miami—she gives examples of the discovery and new directions established through such story sharing. She also explores teaching experiences, even with a group of business executives, about how story sharing around generosity and welcome transform communities of practice.

Tim Shapiro, longtime pastor and now director of the Indianapolis Center for Congregations, reflects in chapter 6 on the way local stories in congregations become sacred stories. He reflects on how most congregations have a key story character and storyteller, like "Geneva" in a church he served. These people embody and pass on the informal stories of members in hallways and meetings, which are as important to the life of a congregation as any official narrative. Shapiro draws on the narrative theory of Stephen Crites to reflect on how narratives constitute human experience as they place temporal and mundane stories in relation to enduring, sacred ones. He gives palpable examples of each kind of story in local congregations and literature, stressing the importance of all forms of storytelling as vehicles of the sacred. Like Scripture, there are a variety of story forms in churches. In the end, these testimonies are "narrated practices" that constitute the heart and soul of a congregation's life. Shapiro ends by sharing ways in which leaders can encourage and learn from such stories in their own communities.

In chapter 7, Niles Goldstein, rabbi of a new synagogue in lower Manhattan, offers a narrative reflection on the state of Jewish life in the city after 9/11. He begins with a remembrance of the immediate aftermath of the tragedy, including the displacement, homelessness, and spiritual dislocation that members of his congregation shared with their neighbors. He raises the key question of what synagogue life, and by implication religious life more generally, means for young urbanites in a city that has experienced radical loss and transition. Judaism itself is filled with resources from scripture and tradition that help communities to cope with such dislocation and change. Goldstein suggests that congregations must re-invent themselves as sanctuaries of safety and community instead of relying on inherited forms of institutional life or membership that have less meaning. Jewish life is well positioned to resist the vapid materialism and individualism of American society by reinventing tradition with new forms of religious expression. To bring that about, rabbis and others must share innovative leadership, which as Rabbi Goldstein's essay exemplifies, must include the ability to hear and nurture stories that navigate change with promise.

This collection ends with a capstone essay by Diana Butler Bass, historian, educator, and congregational researcher. She outlines the parameters of her recent research into vital congregations and religious practices. Then she summarizes four claims about the importance of narrative to this vitality. First, the story one chooses shapes the leadership one can offer: are we leading churches like the Titanic or the Mayflower? Second, stories shape leaders as effective leaders learn the stories of their congregations, encourage people to share those stories, and help navigate or shift those stories, especially in times of chaos. Third, narrative leadership is marked by a leader's ability to take on a character in the community's story by linking his or her own story to that of the community in life-giving ways. Finally, narrative leadership is marked by an authenticity of spiritual practice, which issues in a kind of charisma that is not personality driven, but gift-driven. All of this allows leaders "to create story and to act in concert with the tale."

I trust these gifted practitioners and teachers will inspire your own work to embody, cultivate, and envision new narratives for ministry in your congregations and local community.

Larry A. Golemon
Director
The Alban Institute Narrative Leadership Project

CHAPTER I

The Practice of Narrative Leadership in Ministry

~

LARRY A. GOLEMON

The turn to narrative theory and practice has risen dramatically in a range of professions and academic fields in recent years. Distinct narrative approaches have been developed in education, counseling, and business; anthropology, literary theory, and history; hermeneutics, theology, and ethics. Leading psychologists and educators, such as Jerome Bruner and Howard Gardner, have turned toward narrative analysis in their assessment of education, culture, and leadership. Michael White and David Epston developed narrative therapy, which affected a range of psychotherapy, clinical, and pastoral practices. Business consultants like Stephen Denning have integrated narrative practices into the art of organizational management. Clifford Geertz and William Labov brought interpretive and narrative approaches to cultural analysis and anthropology. Structuralists like Roland Barthes brought new sophistication to the literary theory of narrative, and poststructuralists like Jacques Derrida and Julia Kristeva exposed the semiotic difference and abjection of most Western narratives. Historians like Hayden White have claimed historical narratives as constructive rather than representational. Schools of narrative hermeneutics, theology, and ethics have been developed by the distinctive approaches of Paul Ricoeur and Hans Frei.[1]

The narrative turn in the human sciences has been spawned, in part, by a growing distrust of technical and positivist approaches to answer the deeper questions of human meaning. Bill Sullivan of the Carnegie Foundation for the Advancement of Teaching speaks of the "end of the technical paradigm" of the professions and a turn to more humanistic, narrative forms of professional education. Ron Heifetz speaks of the crucial difference between technical management—built around problem solving and efficiency—and "adaptive leadership," which includes more imaginative and narrative forms. Ministry and theological studies are natural allies in this turn to narrativity, and tremendous work has been done in biblical exegesis, homiletics, pastoral counseling, liturgy, and religious education. But to date, the developments in narrative theory and practice—both within ministry and beyond—have not been brought together in a comprehensive framework for the leadership that pastors, lay leaders, and congregations as a whole can exercise in helping people and the community find deeper meaning in these chaotic times.[2]

The rise of narrative theory and practice is also due to the decline of master narratives from modern culture and religion, including those about the autonomous self, the march of science and progress, and benevolent expansion of wealth and consumer culture. As these narrative worlds have fragmented, new forces of globalization have risen to compete with them. These forces—like worldwide media and communication, transnational immigration, global finance, and the proliferation of technology—create new narratives of global culture that impinge upon local communities. Yet, some theorists of globalization, such as Arjun Appadurai, claim that even this new culture, filled with media dreams of consumer prosperity, are rather thin narratives, which must connect with local communities and cultures to be adapted and reframed. The real narrative work, he claims, lies in the "narrative imagination" of local communities to blend global messages with their own more vibrant local cultures and practices. The tug-of-war between the global and the local for capturing the narrative imagination is intense and everyday, especially in our electronically mediated world.[3]

At the Alban Institute, we believe that even as the narratives of modern Western culture have declined, individuals and communities around the globe continue to form narratives about life's basic questions and challenges. Even in the tug-of-war between global media and local culture, transnational ideologies and popular religions, global economics and local production, individuals around the world still work hard to piece together some meaningful life story. In the context of this global, if not postmodern, flux, we believe the moral philosopher Charles Taylor is right when he claims, "Life has to be lived as a story."[4]

While the fields of theology and ministry have utilized narrative frameworks and methods—from biblical studies, theology, and ethics to homiletics, pastoral care, and congregational studies—the potential of an overarching narrative framework for ministry has yet to be tapped. At Alban, we have been engaged in a Narrative Leadership project, made possible by the Luce Foundation, from 2005 to 2008, exploring the power of story retrieval, reconstruction, and presentation as a framework for ministry, leadership, and congregational change. Through consultations with pastors, lay leaders, seminary educators, and local congregations, we have developed a framework for narrative leadership that we observe in vibrant, life-giving ministries. This chapter reviews the characteristics of narrative leadership in ministry—particularly from the point of view of how it is practiced. Specifically, I describe here the primary *intentions of narrative leadership*, which inform and give shape to various practices of change and renewal in ministry and congregational leadership. These "intentions" build upon the larger framework of "principles" described in the opening chapter of *Teaching Our Story*, another book in Alban's narrative leadership series.

Taken together, we believe the principles and these intentions have the potential to transform contemporary understandings of ministry and congregational life.

The Intentions of Narrative Work by Pastors, Leaders, and Congregations

~

How does good narrative work—the retrieval, construction, and performance of valued stories—take place in ministry? Through consultations and congregational studies, we have identified several key *intentions of narrative leadership* that inform the story work of pastors, lay leaders, and congregations. This multilayered, story work is characterized by the ongoing retrieval, construction, and performance of narratives in all arenas of ministry and congregational life—from sermons and worship to pastoral care to education and mission. Our thesis is that the more pastors, leaders, and congregations exercise these narrative intentions with care, the richer and more generative of change their stories of faith become. The intentions of narrative leadership by pastors, leaders, and congregations are summarized as:

+ Living and sharing God's story as leaders
+ Hearing people's stories and linking them to God's story
+ Creating a community of storytellers and actors
+ Reframing traditions and the past for a healthy future
+ Engaging the world's stories with stories of faith
+ Discerning God's call to a new story in this place
+ Embodying the congregation's new story in renewed practices

Our description of these narrative intentions of pastors, leaders, and congregations begins with the person of the leader and moves outward toward other people, the congregation, and the larger society, then back again to the heart of congregational vision and practices. Pastors and leaders, however, may enter this movement anywhere along the path, depending on the context and present situation faced by their congregation. Congregations and their leaders may specialize in three or four of these intentions, but all seven can be cultivated in most churches and synagogues over time. In the end, the seven intentions of narrative work inform and reinforce one another to create communities of faith that are story formed and forming in all they do.

Living and Sharing God's Story as Leaders

Pastors and other leaders who know their own story with God are better equipped to share God's story with others. If Henry James was right, that "stories happen to people who know how to tell them,"[5] then pastors and leaders who learn to narrate their own spiritual journey—from coming to faith to the call and journey of ministry—develop the story-building capacity to relate God's story in personal terms. Numerous methods already exist for developing spiritual autobiography.[6] Pastors in our project often developed the art of self-narration, often using such tools as a resource for their preaching, pastoral care, and leadership. Whether a leader is intentional or not about retrieving and using his or her spiritual journey, we believe that in many cases the leader's ministry imitates the leader's own storied past.

The themes, values, and priorities of ministry grew out of the spiritual and life journeys of many pastors in our project. Their stories are used by permission.

+ Rev. Scott Colglazier of Riverside Church, New York, twenty years ago spent a powerful retreat in Big Sur, California, with a devotee of Thomas Merton. The theme was "Finding Your Myth," and it was so powerful that he claims, "I can chart much of my life coming from that one-week experience." Colglazier once saw the Christ story as "the *true* story" with which everyone should align, but after that retreat experience he began to see Christ as the "story [that] exists only to unlock our own story. . . . We may point to Jesus, but then he points back to us!" Colglazier does share this story quite openly as it frames much of his ministry around bringing the stories of individuals to intersect with the story of Jesus in a way that changes people.

+ Rev. Anne Durboraw, of St. Luke's Lutheran Church in New Windsor, Maryland, struggled with balancing her ministry with her vocation as a mother after her children were born. She found great solace and inspiration in the tradition of Mary as *theotokos*, or God bearer, because there she realized that "love flows for my children . . . ; and that love is always overflowing, because it comes from God." She learned to trust that enough love and energy would be available for both her family and the congregation. Anne has told this story in her preaching, as a way to inform her congregation of her own sense of multiple vocations and as a way to draw women and men into seeing their parenting as a call given by God.

+ Rev. H. Beecher Hicks Jr. of Metropolitan Baptist in Washington, D.C., was first called to that church when it was struggling with aging congregants and an inadequate building that "smelled like liniment." He began to explore the possibility of moving, and a conflict arose. At one meeting, someone moved his dismissal and someone else adjournment, but he insisted the issue be faced and discussed. After the storm (and the decision to move), he sat down a wrote his book *Preaching Through a Storm*, which tells his journey as pastor during this turbulent time. Because he placed his struggle alongside the congregation's and the larger story of the people of God in Scripture, he concluded, "A story is always connected to a [larger] journey, which ends when the Lord says so."

+ Rev. Doug Liston of New Life Methodist in Wheeling, West Virginia, recounts his early experience of home-lessness, addiction, and recovery as a journey of miracles and healing. "Living on the streets taught me that God is real and changes lives." Doug does tell this story with sensitivity and care, in preaching and other contexts, to help people get in touch with the reality of God's grace and its power to change even them. His humility, disarm-ing candor, and belief in new life inform his own min-istry of listening, dialogue, and healing as several small parishes decide to consolidate into a larger ministry and united church.

These pastors have learned to narrate their own journey with God, and then use that story as a foundation if not a resource for their own ministries. Even when the stories of one's spiri-tual life journey are not openly revealed to the community, they can provide a powerful template for reflecting upon and shaping one's ministry.

Professors of preaching have long debated the pros and cons of leaders' personal sharing from the pulpit; but lately there has been a renewed appreciation of the appropriate use of the pas-tor's own testimony in preaching. Anna Carter Florence, homi-letics professor and author of *Preaching as Testimony*, reported in our project how testimony helps her students "live authenti-cally into the text." Long part of many African American and white evangelical traditions, preachers' testimony is a mark of their faith's authenticity and a bridge to reach the people. Rev. Elizabeth Braxton of Burke Presbyterian Church in north-ern Virginia claims, "People can connect to the pastor's story as the bridge or connection with the biblical story." Beecher Hicks reflects upon writing a book about a difficult time in his ministry: "Telling my story was cleansing; sharing what is on the heart was a release to the congregation so they could

share what was on theirs." Rev. N. Graham Standish of Calvin Presbyterian Church outside of Pittsburgh expresses this
newer trend when he says, "We were told not to share personal
stories in seminary. But now I feel the opposite. The teachers I
liked best were teachers who tell stories, also about themselves.
I have to tell those stories too to grow spiritually; I have to tell
my story—especially of how I failed or was tested or of God
bringing me back. The rule is: you can't be the hero of the story. Larger churches idolize the pastor; so it's important to tell
stories of foibles too."[7]

One pastor told us how she brought a recent life struggle
into the pulpit, as a witness to the resurrection. Rev. Emily Berman D'Andrea, of Lewinsville Presbyterian in northern Virginia, recounted how her fifteen-month-old son took ill during
one Holy Week, and when she took him to the doctor, the staff
rushed him to the hospital due to a serious case of pneumonia.
She continued, "As I'm sitting there holding this child hooked
up to the oxygen, the IV, the antibiotics; and he's just kind of
there, I'm thinking, *Do I really believe this Easter Story? Where is
the good news, the new life?* . . . because my thoughts were going
to the worst-case scenario. I'm thinking, *I can't preach on Easter,* and was starting to think I should have [the other pastor]
preach because I was caring for this little guy."

After her son began to improve on Good Friday and her
extended family arrived to help, she decided to preach, in part
from this experience—a moment where life and Scripture
intersected for her. "I ended up preaching on Easter of my
struggle to believe in the resurrection. It was helpful for me to
recognize that I was living out this biblical story of Holy Week
while I'm in the hospital with my son. Only then did I recognize that God is taking this child, no matter what happens, and
God's own child went through this darkness and then new life
on Easter. The new insight that came is that the biblical story
broadens our own story and gives our story that true meaning."
D'Andrea's decision to preach from the story of accompanying
her son during Holy Week connected her more closely with

Jesus's story and demonstrated how others might broaden their own stories through such connection.

The leader's choice of genre and redemptive motifs for recounting pastoral journeys of faith is crucial to how a congregation identifies with or utilizes them. If a pastor comes across as a hero of tragic proportions, that limits the degree to which people identify with the story, but if he or she comes across as comic discovery and humility, then other doors open up. Standish, author of *Humble Leadership*, has his own rule for self-disclosure in the pulpit: "One can never be the hero of the story."[8] How pastors frame their role during a conflict is key: Is he or she living out the role of a tragic martyr? A comic figure repeating errors? An ironic character of unresolved paradox? Or a nonanxious narrator of whatever genre plots unfold? The redemptive motifs a leader draws upon are crucial to how well a congregation can hear or embrace redemptive choices during a hardship. Will they be invited to seek forgiveness of past wrongs, reconciliation with wrongdoers, emancipation from sacred cows or stuck narratives, or healing from shared loss and grief? How well a pastor or leader embodies and relates redemptive motifs may help the congregation find new choices of hope. Only then can a narrative leader point to the larger, sacred drama that enfolds them. As Hicks says, "One's story is always connected to a larger journey, and it ends when the Lord says so!"

Hearing People's Stories and Linking Them to God's Story

The second intention of narrative leadership in the work of pastors, leaders, and congregations is to link people's stories to others' stories and to God's story. This intention applies most clearly to pastoral care and conversations, but it also extends to small group work, education, and preaching and worship.

Exercising this intention requires the skills of deep or holy listening in pastoral care and spiritual direction, as pastors and leaders listen for the signs of human longing and the stirrings of God's Spirit.[9] Part of such listening includes a kind of narrative listening for the recurring themes, plots, actors, and choices that are part of the person's or family's life. Pastoral theologian Donald Capps writes, "I believe that what makes the narrative approaches . . . valuable and useful for counseling in the congregational context is that they invite us—as pastors—to reflect on how we 'story' our own lives and those of the persons to whom we seek to be of some assistance." Contemporary research in personal narratives shows that people who get stuck in crises often tell the story in a passive, first-person voice about bad things "happening" to them without any choice, while those who move beyond challenges describe them in a more active and reflective voice, even in the third person, that finds new opportunities and choices in hardship. Focused story listening and inquiry in pastoral care can help people re-story their lives with a new sense of direction and purpose.[10]

Religious educator Anne Streaty Wimberly has identified a "story linking method" that uses biblical and black tradition narratives to help people reframe their personal stories. The process begins by inviting personal storytelling through leader disclosure, case studies, paired storytelling by participants, and structured reflection. Then it moves through biblical reflections that use Scripture as a mirror of one's life context. Participants enter the story as one of its characters, and they reflect upon what the story says about God's work here and now. The process continues with stories of liberation from the African American tradition (or any cultural stories of redemption), which are engaged through dramatic readings, group conversation, and reflection. In the end, participants are invited to discern and decide what God is calling them to do as "liberating wisdom" that can illumine their own life path. Most notable, perhaps, is the social nature of the entire process, as story linking brings participants together through their life stories and interpretations of the tradition and creates a learning community focused on discipleship.[11]

Many pastors and leaders in the Alban project sought to
deepen people's stories by linking them with biblical narratives. Some knew of Wimberly's method and have used it in
their teaching or ministry, while others made links intuitively
through their own pastoral practice. Anne Durboraw used
the occasion of a nonmember's funeral to help link a local
working-class family more closely with the gospel. She describes her own listening to this family as they spoke about
the woman and her difficult suicide. Durboraw shared her
intuitions about linking this event to a Gospel account about
Jesus, in this way:

When I met with the family a few days before the service,
they shared with me the story of how this woman loved to
fish. One time she had been fishing all day and had caught
nothing. And when she was packing up to go, she left her line
at the shore and the fishing pole took off into the water. She
chased after it and caught a huge catfish—the biggest of her
life! The obvious story that came to my mind is the story in
Luke 5:1–11 of Jesus calling the first disciples. In particular,
this story is touching because when Jesus calls Peter, Peter
says, "Go away from me Lord, for I am a sinful man!" I pointed out to those gathered at the funeral that day that it was interesting Jesus didn't choose his first disciples from the crowd
of good synagogue-going folk who had followed him to the
shore of the lake. Rather, he chose these fishermen at the bottom of the pay scale. He chose Peter, and even after Peter's
admission that he was a sinful man, Jesus says to him, "Do
not be afraid; from now on you will be fishing for people." In
the homily, I shared the story of this woman's big catch and
related it to this Bible story in Luke. These 175 unchurched
folks were hearing perhaps for the first time, that Jesus calls
imperfect people, sinful people, fearful people. . . . The words
of Jesus, "Do not be afraid," were precisely what this family in
grief and guilt needed to hear. And perhaps it reminded them
that their wife, mother, sister, and friend, even in her own sin

and sadness, heard the precious words of Jesus, "Do not be afraid."[12]

The pastor used the activity of fishing and the class status of the disciples to make direct connections with this family and the wider assembly. By joining the biblical story and the woman's story, she helped this family and their friends hear the word of God: "Be not afraid." This word of comfort and hope reframes the despair of suicide and the difficult grief that follows into a forward-looking framework of healing. While the family never joined a church, Durboraw believes the story must have "touched their souls," because they showed up the next week for worship and continued to attend intermittently for some time.

Two ready-made venues for linking personal stories with God's are prayer and worship liturgies. In *Mighty Stories, Dangerous Rituals*, authors Herb Anderson and Ed Foley make a powerful case for bringing together the narrative work of pastoral care with narrative recital in ritual and worship. Through this intersection, human and divine stories are woven together in new ways: "God has chosen to coauthor a redemptive story for us and with us in human history, and in so doing has invited us to reshape radically the horizon of all other storytelling and ritual making."[13]

Graham Standish shared an account how the acts of confession and communion linked a parishioner with Jesus in new ways. Shirley (not her real name) had a long history with new age and Eastern spirituality, but at a low point in her life, the pastor suggested she "try confession" by first writing down all the things that "kept her away from God." She agreed, and began several weeks of a tearful, numbing, and vulnerable process that left her, in her words, "open and raw." She recalled:

> When I finished I met with Graham in his office. I read the list, and as I did I cried and shook and felt like I was being

emptied. I shook so hard that Graham had to hold my arm. Afterwards, we walked outside and into the church's labyrinth. As we walked, we prayed. At the center of the labyrinth, we burned the paper listing my sins. Then we walked back out praying, went back into Graham's office, and Graham served me communion ... at my suggestion ... and I was so grateful for communion. I felt empty and weak, but I also felt filled with the body of Christ, my Jesus. I had confessed my sins, exposed my sin; and I was forgiven and washed clean by the blood of Jesus. Immediately I started to sense Jesus as a true, real, and living person—my sweet, sweet Jesus. I guess I had to go into the wilderness to find the home of my soul.

Soon after this cleansing confession and nourishing communion, Shirley was commissioned as a healer in the congregation. A new spiritual ministry and path had begun, this time with Jesus at her side. The healing rituals of the church, in this case, bonded Shirley more closely with Christ and allowed him to enter her spiritual narrative as a new and major character.

Weaving human stories with God's story is a natural, intuitive process for many pastors and congregational leaders. By becoming more intentional about this narrative work, pastors and leaders can invite people to identify with their own biblical and faith narratives and reframe aspects of their own lives— from hardship to hope—as part of God's ongoing story with God's people. Part of that reframing comes by connecting our sense of human relevance with a larger purpose or promise of God's time. Sometimes getting outside the stuck story of despair or unresolved healing by reframing these events in light of biblical narratives creates new genres of rising above tragedy or of romantic self-fulfillment that offer redemptive possibilities. How the deep work of stories affects human hearts is, in the end, up to God's Spirit, but narrative leaders can juxtapose and weave stories in ways that creates optimal conditions for the Spirit to be seen and heard.

Creating a Community
of Storytellers and Actors

The third intention of narrative leadership in ministry is creating a community of storytellers and actors within and beyond the congregation. Some congregations cultivate this by creating opportunities for personal testimony, perhaps "the most democratic—and powerful—of all Christian practices." Lillian Daniel writes how testimony changed the lives and congregation of a once-declining New England parish: "After we tell God's story, it tells us, and then we have a new story to tell. The stories shape the community, and the community returns with new stories. But both the telling and the hearing have the power to transform."[14]

Once the province of evangelical and African American churches, testimony is now a practice in many congregations of the old mainline. Whether one calls this practice "testimony" or a "Time for Sharing," as Amazing Grace Lutheran Church in East Baltimore does, it has the power to link people's stories of faith and build up the community, even across old barriers of age, race, and class. Deaconess Katherine Kluckman-Ault describes how practices of testimony at Amazing Grace have helped African Americans claim a new voice in the church, while European Americans and others have adopted this "new" practice with joy. By creating regular venues for personal testimony about how God is at work in people's lives, "storying" one's faith can become a regular part of congregational life and helps create a community of storytellers who act on their faith.

Testimony can also be communicated in written forms. At Calvin Presbyterian Church, Zelienople, Pennsylvania, the yearly spiritual reading guide for Lent has become a powerful tool for witnessing to God's work in personal, life-giving ways. One couple wrote about a journey of fear and discovery occasioned by a health crisis with their two-month-old daughter.

After several experiences with the baby's troubled breathing, they finally rushed her to the emergency room early one morning, only to learn that she needed an emergency breathing tube, probably for the next twelve to eighteen months. Because air no longer flowed through her voice box, the worst part for the parents was that they "could not hear her cry."

This couple's experience of their daughter's crisis was transformed by their experience of community. As they struggled spiritually, to the point of "being in the desert," they became more open to the community's prayer and support, which gathered around them. Their daughter's condition "drew people together"—family, church, and friends—into a new community of healing that embodied God's grace. The mother recalls, "We were connected to the healing team at Calvin. Although we had been praying, our healer from the church helped us to focus our energy on believing that we could help to heal Grace by truly letting go. She said on her first visit that she knew [our daughter] would be healed well before her first birthday." By the time of her second checkup, their daughter's condition was clearing up at an amazing rate, and the physician said her breathing tube could be removed at an unprecedented five months! He added, amazed, "You must be going to the right church." The mother recalls that she had never before felt God's presence as on that day: "I was overcome with a feeling of complete well-being and calm." Being open to signs of support and healing and joining others in prayerful care allowed this family to take an experience of tragic hardship and reframe it as a story of redemption and hope.

Another pastor in our study, Rev. Mike Mather of Broadway United Methodist, Indianapolis, described how his congregation cultivates neighborhood storytelling in order to build relationships, celebrate gifts, and mobilize people around common interests. At the core of this narrative work lies the profound belief that the Holy Spirit is already present and active in people's lives. The church sees its mission to bear witness to that presence by cultivating people's gifts, but it had to restructure itself according to this purpose:

> Key to this new structure was having the Committee on Lay Leadership (CLL), which had most often functioned as the Nominating Committee in the past, take on a new role. Its responsibility is that each member of the committee was asked to have at least five conversations a month with people in and around the life of the congregation. Then when the committee gets together the overwhelming amount of time in the meeting is spent talking together about what the gifts, dreams, passions and stories are of the people they have talked with over the past month. It gives them the opportunity to hear what is happening in the life of the Spirit in the lives of the people of our parish and outside of the parish.

This new mission of listening to "the life of the Spirit in the lives of the people," both within and beyond the church, has reshaped the committee around storytelling and listening. Listening to people's stories for their gifts allows the church to enter a ministry of hospitality and connection, so that people can develop those interests through deeper relationships and shared action.

Broadway Church has hired a "Roving Listener," De'Amon Harges, whose mission is to listen for signs of God's work and call in the lives of community people. The Roving Listener visits people in the community—in hair salons, barbershops, cafes, homes, and other gathering points—to draw out people's life stories, with an ear for naming their gifts and passions as signs of God's call in their lives. For example, De'Amon identified two women in the neighborhood who both loved bicycles, as did a member of the church. Mike recounts, "They came together and had a bike festival this past summer, which included a community-wide bike ride."

By discerning community stories of vocation, Broadway has done more than create communities of common interests. It has also mobilized people for action around key issues in the community. Mather explains, "We have had dinner or evening conversations with an artist group, a health group, a lawyers' group, a gardening group, and a cooks' group. One thing that has come out of that is our local neighborhood has a large group of people who work in health care. A couple of doctors in the congregation have offered to get one-hundred-plus blood pressure cuffs for these health-care folks to take the blood pressures of their neighbors."

The relational focus of such action, however, is what makes Broadway's community organizing and building distinct. Mather emphasizes, the work of the health-care group "is *not* to primarily improve the health of one's neighbors, but to improve connection between neighbors that we believe will result in better health!" Even the church's food pantry ministry asks each person or family that comes to its door these three questions: What are three things you do well enough that you could teach someone else to do them? What three things would you like to learn? and, Who besides God and yourself is going with you along the way? By using each of its ministries as a place of story gathering, Broadway cultivates a language of gifts and God's call as a means for building up the community.

The Broadway United Methodist story includes a major reframing of the existing genre of urban decay into one of neighborhood abundance. By initiating a series of narrative practices in and around the parish, the church has helped create a new discourse of gifts, resources, and talents that defies the traditional narrative. By this careful, community-based narrative work, Broadway has generated new conversations and practices of what Robert Putnam calls "social capital," which both bridge from the congregation to the community and bond members of the congregation in a new mission and purpose.[15] Over time, the congregation's identity—once viewed as a bulwark of like-minded people in a decaying neighborhood—has been transformed, in Mather's words, "into a meeting place of shared dreams." By cultivating a community of listeners, storytellers, and actors all responding to God's call, Broadway has reshaped its own story and that of its community from one of needs and wants to one of gifts and vocation, richly blessed by God.

Reframing Traditions and the Past for a Healthy Future

The fourth intention of narrative leadership in congregations is to reframe tradition and the past for a healthy future. The flexible and changing nature of stories makes them vulnerable to being manipulated by competing points of view and interests. In times of conflict, struggle, or a breach of faith, for example, the malleable nature of stories can generate rumors, half-truths, and cover-ups as various parties compete for establishing the official version, which silences other less powerful voices. In fact, some stories are told to hide things we don't want others to know about. Just as families who struggle with addiction, violence, or infidelity tell stories to conceal their shame or fear, congregations can establish stories that conceal histories of conflict, sexual misconduct, or financial irresponsibility of which their pastors or other leaders have been a part. Reframing these past stories, and the traditions that accompany them, is a vital part of transformative narrative leadership.

Being intentional about reframing congregational narratives and religious tradition requires both personal and symbolic intelligence, as people invested in old stories must be brought along in order to invest in the newly crafted ones. One of the powerful therapeutic movements today, narrative therapy,[16] employs both intelligences by helping individuals and families identify their stuck narratives and reframe them. The counseling strategies are aimed at deconstructing the "problem-saturated" stories people tell by, first, externalizing the problem, then mapping the influence of the problem over the family, and then identifying the actors' influence over the story through "alternative episodes."[17] Increasingly, narrative therapy is being utilized in pastoral counseling for individuals and families[18] and by Alban church consultants to deconstruct congregational systems. (See *Finding Our Story*, another book in Alban's narrative leadership collection.) It is proving to be a powerful method to help congregations unpack problem stories, identify moments when they broke out of that dominant narrative, and chart new patterns of response for the future. Re-storying the congregation's versions of the past becomes crucial to chart the future.

Reframing a congregation's past often requires facing shameful or hurtful events. Rev. Jean Kuebler, of Big Spring Lutheran Ministry Cooperative, Newville, Pennsylvania, puts it this way: "A congregation can have sick, deceitful stories about its soul. . . . It's not enough for the pastor to name it. There is something larger at stake . . . relationships that are intact; or something scary that causes people to stay stuck." Emily Berman D'Andrea shared how her church finally learned to say a healthy farewell to a faithful pastor after a long history of earlier pastoral scandals:

> The leave-taking of the pastors at Lewinsville Presbyterian Church in its 160-year history had been rocky at best. Every pastor in the congregation's collective memory (except the present head of staff) left because of some scandal, and the departure had been hurtful and bitter. The way the pastor, staff, session, and congregation handled the current pastor's upcoming departure was important for the well-being of the congregation. . . . The congregation needed to tell stories about what was and is good. They needed to celebrate in the midst of their grief over the thought of losing a beloved pastor.

Through a congregation-wide process, leaders and members shared the strengths, discoveries, and accomplishments of this long pastorate, and members learned to replace the old expectation of troubled pastorates with new, healthier expectations. Telling stories of recent pastoral accomplishments and gifts helped create this new expectation.

Kuebler told how the history of various churches that went into forming Big Spring Cooperative Ministry had to be reframed by key lay leaders to help a consolidation process. A "pivotal town meeting" of more than two hundred people—most of them anxious about the future—was held, during which several lay people retrieved stories of the past in constructive ways. One lay leader recalled how the closing of one-room schoolhouses to form a consolidated district high school created great anxiety in the 1940s, but the benefits of more resources, better facilities, and extended community convinced everyone over time that this was the right move. Another man, one of the carpenters in the community, retrieved a bit of denominational history as a guide for the future:

> In a very down-to-earth way, he reminded us of the longer and larger history of the Lutheran church in South-Central Pennsylvania. He reminded us of the circuit-rider days, and how churches were planted across the Cumberland Valley as the settlements kept moving west. He reminded us of how the original impulse was not so much about having buildings but about spreading the gospel, and how the buildings were always meant to be a means to that end. He reminded us how, over the centuries, congregations have moved to new facilities, congregations have grown and died, but that the church has gone on. He helped us to see our particular hopes and anxieties about a new church in the context of a much larger story about mission.

These lay leaders retrieved snapshots of denominational history and local school consolidation to reinforce the missional focus, resiliency, and accrued benefits of the community in times of change. These reclaimed assets helped move forward the consolidation of some of the churches.

One story of cooperative ministry and eventual consolidation deserves special attention. Doug Liston had a vision for

consolidating declining and disconnected Methodist congregations in the coal-mining city of Wheeling, West Virginia. He
described the challenge presented by local history this way:

> There were many boundaries to cross and barriers to tear
> down. One congregation was the remnant of a hard working,
> hard living, hard fighting neighborhood where the parents
> worked in the mills and the children stayed with grandpar-
> ents. Another congregation was the remnant of a Scottish
> and Irish middle-class, white-collar neighborhood that is
> now multicultural and marked by increasing unemployment,
> drugs, and violence. Another congregation was the remnant
> of the white, German, upper-class, business owners' neigh-
> borhood, where the homes, once elegant, large, and luxurious,
> are now low-rent apartments occupied by racially and cultur-
> ally mixed families. Another congregation was largely upper-
> middle-class, professional African American with a scattering
> of white spouses and recently received white families.

The history of each congregation, and the denominational mission patterns by which they were founded, created what Liston
called "rigid boundaries along ethnic, cultural and economic
lines," which had to be overcome. The pastor initiated joint
worship services, introduced community meetings to a "Mutual Invitation" process for sharing and listening, and developed
a joint ministry council of leaders from each congregation.[19]
In time, the pastor, congregations, and leaders "set out upon a
long and arduous course of 'coming together,' a gradual process
of socialization and re-patterning of shared assumptions about
the worship life and mission of the Church. New relationships
were forged and old friendships renewed."

Liston's use of mutual invitation allowed for congregational
stories to be revisited and reevaluated at a very personal level.
This process, developed by Eric Law for multicultural contexts,
invites each person in a group to speak in turn, until all voices

are heard. Gradually, the congregational members and leaders built connections, renewed trust, and a mutual process of healing around their shared stories of the glory days, congregational decline, and hoped-for renewal:

> They shared first their best memory of their church: stories of the glory days and packed houses, stories of beloved Sunday school teachers, stories of chicken dinners, playing hide-and-seek after the lights were turned out, stories of being the "heathen" neighborhood children who were welcomed by the church. One at a time, they journeyed through the past. Tears were shed; laughter broke out. Together, they began to see a common thread and to view each other from a different perspective. . . . In the weeks and months of meetings that followed, they were asked to share stories of their worst experiences in church, their saddest times, their toughest decisions, and their most painful mistakes—stories that increased in degrees of personal intimacy as levels of shared trust increased. Gradually, they constructed a common narrative and realized they were each part of a larger story—a shared and binding story, a sacred story.

The birthing of New Life United Methodist Church through community-based storytelling allowed older histories of ethnic and class distinction to be set aside in favor of a new, collaborative narrative of revitalization.

By rehearsing, sifting through, and reframing inherited congregational stories, pastors, leaders, and members learn to set aside problem-saturated versions of the past, celebrate moments of breaking out of these legacies, and reclaim healthy, promising versions of their congregational story. Both personal and symbolic intelligence are key as people must be involved in identifying breakaway moments in their past that lay the imaginative seed for a newer, healthy story. Numerous methods, including narrative therapy and mutual invitation, are available to rehearse, weigh, and find healthy versions of the past through collaborative, community-based action. Pastors' and leaders' intentionality about which methods are used, with whom, and how they create an imaginative space for healthy versions of the past are marks of good narrative leadership.

Engaging the World's Stories with Stories of Faith

The fifth intention of narrative leadership for pastors and congregations is that of engaging the world's stories with stories of faith. Congregations can choose a range of responses— from prophetic critique to cultural co-opting—as part of their faithful narrative work. The global and multistoried universe we live in, with its constant flow of information, paradigms, and practices between a variety of cultures, requires a more sophisticated set of options today than ever before.

One model of forming the narrative imagination in this age of globalization comes from theorist Arjun Appadurai mentioned above. He describes various global forces that impinge upon local communities, including the flows of global media (*mediascapes*), technology (*technoscapes*), finance (*financescapes*), immigration (*peoplescapes*), and belief systems (*ideoscapes*). Each of these flows generates narratives that seek to legitimate its reach into various sectors and quarters of human life.[20] Hollywood movies, for example, encircle the globe with a narrative promise of the American dream; the World Wide Web promotes ready access to the global village; and global financial systems promise consumer abundance. Local communities do not simply swallow these narratives whole, however, as they co-opt them to serve their own local narratives and interests. Bollywood films, for example, recast Hollywood motifs into epic Indian romances; Muslim communities utilize the Web to promote Islamic revivalism locally; and microfinancing reframes global economics to serve local community production. To capture global flows for local interests, Appadurai says a community must exercise narrative imagination that allows it to recast global narratives for local meaning and abundance.

Some congregations decide to confront the worldly challenges that surround them by developing a narrative imagination that is prophetic. Beecher Hicks recounts how Metropolitan Baptist Church began "in the Hell's Bottom neighborhood of D.C., so it has always dealt with all kinds of hell." He has written about his own vision of the preacher's role as prophet and watchperson (Ezek. 33) who rallies the community to heed the dangers around it:

> The watchperson's task is to look over the landscape and alert the city to any approaching danger. The watchperson assures that robbers do not steal the crops before their life-sustaining grains have been harvested and stored in barns. . . . God likewise needs a watchperson. God did so then and does so now. God needs a watchperson—not a politician, not an economic analyst, . . . not a mere reader of Scriptures or reciter of prayers. When the government has little sense of God, when the nation is overcome with institutional greed and moral madness, when the flag waves higher than the cross, and when war is preferred over peace, God requires a watchperson![21]

But the cry of warning must become a vision of ministry in the congregation at large. Metropolitan Baptist Church has embraced the call with a host of ministries that respond to the challenges of modern life around it. The congregation is proactive in strengthening marriage and families, working with youth, addressing sobriety and addiction, ministering and educating around AIDS, and promoting excellence in black education and the professions. One of the greatest challenges has been using narratives and ministries of hope to address the underbelly of cultural and economic forces in the heart of

Washington, D.C., that adversely affect racial difference, local communities, and peace.

Another congregation faced a crisis of globalization—the pandemic of AIDS orphans in Africa—by creating an alternative vision and story for an orphanage with church partners in Kibwezi, Kenya. Elizabeth Braxton of Burke Presbyterian Church shared in a sermon about a "heart-wrenching" story in the *Washington Post* of a nine-year-old girl whose mother "taught [her] how to care for the baby in the family, and the last thing the mother taught her child was how to bury her when she died." She recalled the haunting question of a minister they had worked with in Kibwezi the year before: "What are we going to do with the children all alone showing up at church?" Braxton remembers, "It was as if God was speaking out of those pages to me: 'You need to start an orphanage in Kibwezi.'" But this pastor has a firm belief that such visions must be confirmed "through a convergence of circumstance" if it is a genuine vision from God. Soon she heard from others in the congregation who had read the same article. She shared her vision with the session, who approved a reconnaissance trip to Kibwezi as part of her sabbatical leave. Finally, upon arriving in Kibwezi for a meeting with church partners there, Braxton recalls "being apprehensive because . . . the mission groups from the church have always gone to Kenya as servants to work alongside them. Never had we gone over to tell them something they needed to do." But then the final sign came:

> When I sat down with the persons the director of Kibwezi's Educational Centre, Samuel Mote, had called together to talk about orphan care, I decided to first share my vision. . . . Carol Riitha, who was a community nurse for the AMREF clinic next door, which had just closed, was looking for a job. She told me later . . . that she had been praying to God for work and she wanted her work to have something to do

with children! Carol Riitha was the perfect person to be the Coordinator of the Orphan Care Program.

Braxton says that "God had already paved the way" for this vision to become reality. The orphanage ministry was born and continues to this day. In her preaching, Braxton returns to this story, born of a divine convergence, by linking it to the double vision given separately to Peter and Paul in Acts 11:1–18. There God tells them that the gospel must reach out "beyond the boundary" of established faith practice. Different people, given a similar vision, can give birth to something new and powerful to share with the world. This attentiveness to divine convergences and double visions at work in the people of God is a process that Braxton has come to describe, quite matter of factly, as "Spirit-speak."[22]

Other churches co-opt worldly narratives to strengthen the faith stories they support. Graham Standish is very interested in how narrative plots in popular culture can illumine or be used to enrich faith narratives. He has a special interest in films and reflects on a book by screenwriter Robert McKee:[23]

> I've been fascinated with how the best stories in novels and film always follow a particular pattern of introduction, set-up, crisis, transformation, redemption, and reformation. According to McKee, good stories always reflect a clearly defined plot that follows the patterns of great literature throughout history, including biblical literature. This is especially true of drama that follows the principles of "archplot," where characters encounter some sort of conflict that challenges them. The crisis must be resolved either through the transformation of the environment, which the main character sparks, or through the interior transformation of the main character. The transformation, exterior or interior, eventually leads to the resolution of the conflict, and often to redemption of either the environment or the main character. *Norma Rae* is

an example of exterior transformation; *Thelma and Louise* of interior transformation. *Star Wars* and the *Lord of the Rings* films exhibit both interior and exterior transformation.

Through this movement of set-up, crisis, transformation, and redemption, the dominant story in popular media reflects a heroic genre—either in tragic or romantic form—that emphasizes rising above conflict through lasting transformation.

Standish reflects on the implications of film narratives for congregational leadership and ministry. If congregations adopt the sequel to an older story or if congregations must write their own script anew, they can become blocked in this creative, reenvisioning work: "I've also noticed how ineffective leaders seem to be like authors stuck either in writer's block or in cliched, redundant story lines. Either they can't quite seem to find an alternative path for their story, and they get stuck being unable to move out of crisis, or they lead in a safe, bland way that doesn't lead to transformation." By contrast, effective narrative leaders and their congregations look for ways to rewrite inherited scripts or to shape new ones toward a path of change and transformation:

> Effective leaders find creative ways to script their congregations, and they find alternative plotlines that lead to redemption, reconciliation, and sometimes resurrection. For instance, when I first came to Calvin Presbyterian Church, it [was] a church in the midst of a thirty-year decline, but I recognized the need to lead the church into transformation. The initial challenge was to overcome potential conflict—with staff over what a growing church would mean or with elders about a new focus on prayer and spirituality—with efforts toward transformation. As a leader, I sought ways to overcome a plotline of decline to a plotline of resurrection. In the process, I was always seeking to guide the church to a new story line: one of success and the ability to accomplish what didn't seem possible.

Standish intentionally looks for plotlines in congregations that "follow biblical story lines" of resurrection and redemption. Jesus taught, preached, and healed; met resistance of the worst kind; and overcame it (even in death) to bring new ministry and new life. Similarly, "Congregations can, despite going through a period that feels like it will lead to death, find a way to bring about new life," he reflects. A new congregational story of redemption—both inner and outer—can be created.

By developing a rich narrative imagination in their local congregations, these and other pastors help faith communities respond in new ways to the social and global influences around them. Recasting a former plotline of tragic loss to one of redemptive possibility allows a congregation to forge ahead to a new future. These pastors help place the current ministry and mission of their congregations within the wider horizon of what God is doing in the world. Responding to hellish conditions with new ministries of hope, recasting a plotline of decay into one of resurrections, and reacting to a global crisis of AIDS orphans with a boundary-breaking ministry provide signs of narrative imagination at work in response to the world. These new congregational stories are made possible by the gifted pastoral imagination of congregational leaders who see in the world's events and news the hand of God's work and the call to a new ministry.

Discerning God's Call to a New Story in This Place

The sixth intention of narrative leadership in congregations is to discern God's call to a new story in the congregation's setting. The keys to this work are twofold: first, to build on the strengths and gifts of a congregation and its context, and, second, to create a collective process of discernment, by which all leaders and members are listening for God's guidance and sometimes new direction for the future.

Congregational studies and practice have seen a shift in recent years from a needs-based or challenge-based assessment of a congregation's future mission to an asset-based form of discernment. Drawing from community-development work, congregational consultant Luther Snow argues for identifying the gifts, resources, and strengths of a congregation and its setting as the basis for strategic planning. Most Alban consultants now utilize asset mapping and other strength-oriented methods, such as appreciative inquiry in which members and community stakeholders build upon what they value most about the congregation. No matter how much asset mapping or appreciative inquiry a congregation does, we at Alban believe that clergy, leaders, and their congregations must move from identifying strengths as resources for ministry to a process of discernment around where God is leading this community of faith. Conversation and listening around basic questions such as, Who are we? What has God called us to do or be? and Who is our neighbor? are crucial to shaping a congregation's story in accord with God's unfolding story. Doing so, however, may challenge established canons of identity and tradition.[24]

At Alban, we had the good fortune of walking with a specific congregation during its own mission-vision process in 2007. Burke Presbyterian Church (BPC) in northern Virginia developed an appreciative inquiry process of discernment, which focused on members' storytelling. The congregation trained facilitators, planned a series of neighborhood cottage meetings, and brought people together for conversations around these topics:[25]

1. Remembering your entire experience at our church, tell us a story about when you felt most alive, most motivated and excited about your involvement.
2. When you consider all of your experiences at our church, relate a story about what has contributed most to your *spiritual life*.

3. Tell us a story that illustrates the healthiest, most life-giving aspects of the *relationships among people* at our church.
4. When you think about how our church has related to our *community and the world*, give . . . an example (in detail) as to what you think has been most important.
5. Tell us what you think is the most *important value* that makes our church unique.
6. Make three *wishes for the future* of our church and describe what the church would look like as these wishes come true.

These conversations took place in pairs, then in small groups at two dozen cottage meetings. Both the questions and the informal, relational style embody one of the primary values of this congregation: relational ministry.

The stories and reflections elicited by the discernment process at BPC illustrated a number of core values cherished by members. These included commitments to youth, being welcoming and accepting of all, cultivating a diversity of membership and programs, engaging in mission, focusing on worship in all it does, interfaith work and relations, and the importance of the pastors' interest and involvement with people. What stands out in this storytelling process, however, is how almost every report of spiritual growth, every act of discipleship, every experience of healing love is mediated by the depth of relationships formed in the congregation. Moreover, these relationships are not built around homogeneity but a sense of difference and openness.

Members who attended cottage meetings responded in their own words in these interviews:[26]

+ Members "express the love of God by attending to God's people."
+ "We are people oriented not material oriented."

+ As a newcomer, "I was looking for a small town mentality . . . the personal feeling you get when you walk through the door."
+ "We are truly inclusive and work to be more welcoming to all."
+ "BPC takes people from such a diverse and transient community and creates a cohesive church family."
+ There is "not a clique structure in the church, but there's an interaction and integration that plays well . . . through a philosophy of inclusion."

The discernment process underlines one of the deep practices in this congregation: that ministry is shaped by bringing people together from a diversity of backgrounds into committed relationships. BPC sustains much of this relational energy through a web of small groups and distinct ministries that enhance the practice of discipleship, intimacy, and spiritual growth. Members' responses include:

+ "The Stephen Ministry group was so supportive in my time of need last year as I was trying to be there for my friend."
+ In a small group retreat, "Each person took two hours to share their own journey, resulting in a new depth of relationship."
+ From a women's group: "We've been through the death of a child, the birth of a child, and divorce . . . [as] a support group."
+ "Godly play . . . reaches out to children at the core level."
+ Youth on mission trips "turn away from personal issues and go right to serving the Lord by serving others."

Even the so-called activist ministries in community outreach and homeless ministry foster the sense of discipleship through relationships:

+ At Christ House ministry, "the camaraderie of the men's group as they served together was joyous."
+ "Hypothermia week [with the homeless] was very meaningful for me in relating with those in need; doing something personal for them, touching them."
+ Mission in Kenya: "Kibwezi is really phenomenal and the idea that this relationship has grown [to include] the orphanage and library."

As one member summed up, "The personalized nature of reaching out beyond our walls [includes] . . . face-to-face involvement. . . . People matter to BPC." In short, the stories from the cottage meetings helped the congregation celebrate that ministry is formed relationally at BPC.

One of the gifts of narrative inquiry during a mission-vision process is to articulate the theology of a church in lay terms. BPC members shard theological reflections:

+ "I think the Christians at Burke Presbyterian Church are unique in their ways of relating to one another. You can feel the sense of belonging and commitment in the church activities. . . . In ongoing relationships with other congregations: Jewish and Muslim."
+ "The community of loving relationships we have in our church helps us to love God."
+ "Christ is there and wrapped around you, rather than preached at you."

Christ "wrapped around" the people is a good metaphor for the heart of Burke's life. The church is built around a relational matrix, with God and Christ at the center. There, in face-to-face meetings of sharing, study, friendship, and service, the members forge what the German theologian Dietrich Bonhoeffer called "life together."[27]

The challenge for Burke Presbyterian lies in wanting to grow while not weakening its relational center. After much study, prayer, worship, and conversation, the congregation is developing its own understanding of church growth as a way to move forward. The discernment team passed on to the church board a pair of recommendations that, taken together, reinforce the relational understanding of this new mission and focus: "The Recommendation envisions BPC reaching out into our local community with a combination of evangelism and mission efforts, thereby responding to both the Great Commission in Matthew 28 (to 'make disciples') and the Great Commandment in Matthew 22 (to 'love God and love neighbor'). These two components of the Recommendation are complementary and symbiotic."[28] At BPC, the Great Commission to make disciples is interpreted relationally by extending hospitality to the community. The Great Commandment of loving our neighbor is envisioned as deepening local ties through neighborhood mission. The relational matrix and practices of the congregation—envisioned by members as its highest asset—is seen as the vehicle by which these classic visions of the Christian faith can be moved forward in its context.

Careful discernment is enhanced by rich, personal testimony and interpersonal stories about what matters most in life and in a congregation. The personal and relational texture of the narrative work at BPC illustrates the power of storytelling for discerning from the ground up how God is calling the community's gifts to be used in the future. Tapping the rich narrative capacity of ordinary members is one key to setting up these collaborative storytelling and discernment processes.

Embodying the Congregation's New Story in Renewed Practices

The seventh and final intention of narrative leadership in congregations focuses on embodying the new story in renewed congregational practices. Effective narrative work must engage the social practices of congregations in order to be realized and sustained. Stories in the wider culture—from film, televi-

sion, popular music, magazines, and popular literature—affect
people largely through their immediate impact or emotional
payload; and, in time, they are often forgotten. For narratives to
enter the life of a congregation with lasting impact, they must
inform the social practices of that community. Good narrative
leaders, we have found, revive dormant or routine congregational practices with new narratives, and at times they create
new practices to fully realize a new story.

One model for relating new narratives to congregational
practices is derived from Diana Butler Bass's work on church
practices. Practices are things that congregations "do together
in community that form them in God's love for the world."[29]
Practices in this sense are forms of social interaction that extend the values or goods of the practices to higher levels of
excellence and to more participants, in ways that form them
for service to and with God. The more intentional leaders are
about the way they retrieve, construct, and present narratives,
the more tradition and social practices transform each other.
We believe the narrative work of congregations—through sustained retrieval, construction, and presentation of the stories
of faith—lies at the heart of a renewing relationship between
tradition and social practices. As Bass writes, "Tradition is embodied in practices. And practices convey meaning through
narrative."[30] This dynamic, mutually supporting relationship
between tradition, narratives, and practices can be illustrated as
a circle of generativity:

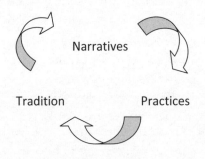

Narratives

Tradition   Practices

At the center of this generative circle lies the imagination of pastors, leaders, and the congregation as they move from tradition through narratives and practices and back again. As Bass puts it, "Imagination is the stage on which narrative, tradition, and practice perform their dance."[31]

Rev. Dr. Sam Lloyd, dean of the Washington National Cathedral, came to the post in 2005. He knew the Cathedral as a grand and beautiful edifice that benefited from a strong endowment and a sense of mission in what he described as "being there for the nation." Presidential funerals, national celebrations, and other events mark its ministry to the nation's capital. While the programs were rich and the worship calendar full (five services a day, eight on Sundays), he soon realized that there was no "we" at the Cathedral in the same sense the adjacent parish church had. Drawing on his doctorate in English literature and his experience in other parishes, he realized that the Cathedral might need a "new narrative to live by" that would help create such a community. So the Cathedral Chapter invited Lloyd to begin a process that would help them discern a new story for their future.

Over time Lloyd and his colleagues laid the foundations of ancient church practices that could be renewed for new narrative inspiration and guidance. He invited the dozen ordained clergy together on a regular basis for prayer, worship, and study. He engaged strategic lay leaders in a series of Bible studies using the African Method of readings, which is based upon "reading, reacting, and responding" with key words and insights about God's call from each participant.[32] He preached regularly on the challenge of community building, especially in an age of competition, market values, and overextension. He invited clergy, lay leaders, and congregants to create a culture of discernment, marked by communal practices of reading, prayer, and worship and open to new images and stories for guidance. After some time, he and the leadership honed in on a passage from 1 Peter: "Come to him, a living stone, though rejected by

mortals yet chosen and precious in God's sight, and like living
stones, let yourselves be built into a spiritual house, to be a holy
priesthood" (1 Peter 2:4–5a).

Because this narrative was rediscovered within the context
of social practices that fostered discernment, it illumined those
practices and gave them new depth and texture. Lay leaders and
clergy began to reflect upon the implications of moving from a
"house of limestone" to one of "living stones" as a new vision for
the National Cathedral. Upon reflection, Lloyd sums up his
ministry this way: "I try to create a metaphor to help people
step inside of." Today the Cathedral's new vision statement
reads, "Now we are engaged in the work of creating an edifice
made of living stones, of human spirits imbued with God's own
Spirit being built into a temple of people and prayers, music
and ministries, committees and communities."[33]

Stories can also flow into congregational practices through
the everyday lives of members. Mike Mather describes how
church practices are holding places for personal stories to be
rehearsed and transformed. He describes one drama between
two strong women in the community, Barb and Ronda. Barb
"struggles with her own violence against others," but in ways
that allow her to recognize others' pain so "the gentleness that
lies underneath . . . is set free." When Mike ran into her in the
sacristy one Sunday, she was preparing communion for that
day, wearing "a dirty black jean jacket, gray sprinkled throughout her black hair, and a fierce expression on her usually kind
face." After communion, which she did not attend, he found
her back in the sacristy cleaning up, and he asked what was
wrong. After pressing her, she finally came out with the story,
which Mather shares in a colloquial fashion:

> The week before she was helpin' out with the meal team [with
> the homeless] and she got mad at one of the guys who kept
> comin' back for more before everybody else was served. she
> was standin' in the kitchen and she cursed him under her
> breath—she says to me, "you know i have a problem with vio-

lence. you know i wanted to go upside his head. but i didn't. i
just said somethin'. i don't think he coulda heard it. but ronda
did." Ronda is workin' in the kitchen too: fiery, fierce, and she's
as willowy as barb is solid. ronda is a peace activist and justice
worker. but barb has just pushed her buttons. barb says to
me, "she got in my face and she tore me up. i never felt that
bad after fightin' with somebody. i lost all my confidence. that
never happened to me before." and the tears spilled down her
tough, rough face. "i don't know whether i can be around here
any more," she said.

Mather spoke to her quietly as people moved in and out of the
sacristy, "giving us space." He gave her words of encouragement,
challenged her, prayed with her. She said, "I was supposed to go
to kids' church this week, but I couldn't. I don't trust myself any
more." Right then another member walked in, and said, "Barb,
i can't be with the kids next week, i'm gonna be gone. can you
take my place?" Mike smiled at Barb and said, "Barb . . . ya gotta
do this . . . It's a sign for sure." Barb looked at her and paused,
Mike held his breath and she said, "i'll try. i can't promise you,
but i'll try."

Mather and the congregation make room for people's stories—like Ronda's struggle with violence—to be rehearsed
and even challenged within the context of church practices,
including its homeless ministry, communion preparation,
and children's ministry. Mather meets people's stories where
they arise—even in the sacristy—and the community "gives
space" for story review, sharing, and reframing. This fluidity
of people bringing their daily stories to church life creates a
culture of openness that allows those stories to be worked out
and the church practices that receive them renewed. Mather
writes, "The next Sunday ronda is one of the ministers of the
cup, and barb is in the house. I wonder whether she'll come to
communion. She does and kneels at the rail in front of ronda.
ronda holds it out, 'the blood of christ for you, barb,' and barb
says, 'amen.'" Social practices of congregations—in liturgy,

hospitality, and elsewhere—can be a holding and healing place for personal stories of conflict, shame, or broken relationship. Allowing these practices to be infused with and reframed by personal narratives revitalizes them as places of human interaction, healing, and reconciliation.

By crafting new metaphors or tapping the stories of congregation members, these pastors have enriched existing practices with narrative power. In turn, these practices—of liturgy, mission, and hospitality—have been renewed and redirected toward the upbuilding of community and relationship among God's people. For congregational practices to become truly collaborative, open, and responsive to new narrative energies requires trusting the creative flow between new stories and renewed practices. Good narrative leaders instill and embody such trust, as congregations begin to embody the stories they believe and cultivate. During one session in Alban's Narrative Leadership project, Diana Butler Bass shared how "re-traditioning" can involve several layers of tradition and history, including the stories of the church's leadership, the local community, and those of the nation and world. Re-traditioning the life of the local church and its theological or denominational heritage is key to the process of revitalizing new congregational practices in this global age.

Begin with Your Congregation's Strengths

⁓

This chapter's description of the narrative work of pastors, leaders, and congregations begins with the person of the leader and moves outward toward other people, the congregation, and the larger society, then back again to the heart of congregational vision and practices. Pastors and leaders, however, may enter this movement anywhere along the path, depending on the situation of the congregation they serve. For some pastor-centered churches, starting with the narratives of the leader may be the right place; for family-size congregations or those dominated by strong personalities, beginning with listening and linking may be best; and for those that have suffered recent conflict, reframing stories of the past may be a better beginning point. In the end, the various intentions of narrative work inform and reinforce one another to create communities of faith that are story formed and forming in all they do. To paraphrase a common line in other fields of practice, "The story must go on," and countless congregations across the nation are engaged in creative and new ways to do just that.

Notes

~

1. Jerome Bruner, *The Culture of Education* (Cambridge, MA: Harvard University Press, 1996); Howard Gardner, *Leading Minds: An Anatomy of Leadership* (New York: HarperCollins, 1996); Michael White and David Epston, *Narrative Means to Therapeutic Ends* (New York: W. W. Norton, 1990); Stephen Denning, *The Leader's Guide to Storytelling: Mastering the Art and Discipline of Business Narrative* (San Francisco: Jossey-Bass, 2005); Clifford Geertz, *The Interpretation of Cultures* (New York: Basic Books, 1973); William Labov, *Sociolinguistic Patterns* (Philadelphia: University of Pennsylvania Press, 1973); Roland Barthes, *The Semiotic Challenge* (Berkeley, CA: University of California Press, 1994); Jacques Derrida, *Writing and Difference*, trans. Alan Bass (London: Routledge and Kegan Paul, 1978); Julia Kristeva, *Powers of Horror: An Essay on Abjection* (New York: Columbia University Press, 1982); Hayden White, *The Content of the Form: Narrative Discourse and Historical Representation* (Baltimore: Johns Hopkins University Press, 1990); Paul Ricoeur, *Time and Narrative*, vols. 1–3 (Chicago: University of Chicago Press, 1984); Hans W. Frei, *Theology and Narrative: Selected Essays* (New York: Oxford, 1993).

2. William Sullivan, *Work and Integrity: The Crisis and Promise of Professionalism in America*, 2nd ed. (San Francisco: Jossey

Bass, 2005); Ron Heifetz, *Leadership Without Easy Answers* (Cambridge: Belknap Press, 1994); David M. Gunn and Danna Nolan Fewell, *Narrative in the Hebrew Bible*, Oxford Bible Series (New York: Oxford University Press, 1993); John R. Donahue, *The Gospel in Parable: Metaphor, Narrative, and Theology in the Synoptic Gospels* (Minneapolis: Fortress Press, 1990); Charles Campbell, *Preaching Jesus: New Directions for Homiletics in Hans Frei's Postliberal Theology* (Grand Rapids: Wm. B. Eerdmans, 1997); David L. Larsen, *Telling the Old, Old Story: The Art of Narrative Preaching* (Grand Rapids: Kregel, 2001); Donald Capps, *Living Stories: Pastoral Counseling in a Congregational Context* (Minneapolis: Fortress Press, 1998); and Donald Miller, *Story and Context: An Introduction to Christian Education* (Nashville: Abingdon, 1988).

3. Arjun Appadurai, *Modernity at Large: Cultural Dimensions of Globalization*, Public Worlds, vol. 1 (Minneapolis: University of Minnesota Press, 1996).

4. Charles Taylor, *Sources of the Self: The Making of the Modern Identity* (Cambridge, MA: Harvard University Press, 1989), 289.

5. Attributed to James by Jerome Bruner in "Life as Narrative," *Social Research* 54, Fall 2004, 1–17.

6. James Fowler, "Faith Development Interview," in *Stages of Faith: The Psychology of Human Development and the Quest for Meaning* (San Francisco: Harper and Row, 1981); Ira Progoff, *At a Journal Workshop: Writing to Access the Power of the Unconscious and Evoke Creative Ability* (New York: Tarcher, 1992); and James Newby, *Gathering the Seekers* (Herndon, VA: Alban Institute, 1995), online at http://www.congregationalresources.org/Seekers/Home.asp.

7. John M. Buchanan, "The 'I' in Sermons," *The Christian Century*, March 6, 2007, FindArticles.com (accessed June 30, 2007); Anna Carter Florence, *Preaching as Testimony* (Louisville, KY: Westminster John Knox, 2007); H. Beecher Hicks, *Preaching Through a Storm* (Grand Rapids: Zondervan, 1987).

8. N. Graham Standish, *Humble Leadership: Being Radically Open to God's Guidance and Grace* (Herndon, VA: Alban Institute, 2007).

9. Susan K. Hedahl, *Listening Ministry: Rethinking Pastoral Leadership* (Minneapolis: Fortress Press, 2001); Margaret Guenther, *Holy Listening: The Art of Spiritual Direction* (Cambridge, MA: Cowley, 1992).

10. Janet Ruffing, *Uncovering Stories of Faith: Spiritual Direction and Narrative* (New York: Paulist Press, 1989); Edward P. Wimberly, *African American Pastoral Care* (Nashville: Abingdon, 1991); Andrew D. Lester, *Hope in Pastoral Care and Counseling* (Louisville, KY: Westminster John Knox, 1995); Donald Capps, *Living Stories: Pastoral Counseling in Congregational Context* (Minneapolis: Fortress Press, 1998); Dan P. McAdams, *The Redemptive Self: Stories Americans Live By* (New York: Oxford University Press, 2005).

11. Anne Streaty Wimberly, *Soul Stories: African American Christian Education*, rev. ed. (Nashville: Abingdon, 2005), 54.

12. This quotation and others in this chapter, unless otherwise cited, come from written summaries and interviews offered by participants in the Alban Institute's Narrative Leadership project.

13. Herbert Anderson and Edward Foley, *Mighty Stories, Dangerous Rituals: Weaving Together the Human and the Divine* (Jossey-Bass, 1998), 37.

14. Diana Butler Bass, *Christianity for the Rest of Us: How the Neighborhood Church Is Transforming Faith* (San Francisco: HarperSanFrancisco, 2006), 134; Lillian Daniel, "Speaking Faith: Grace Breaking In," in *From Nomads to Pilgrims: Stories from Practicing Congregations* (Herndon, VA: Alban Institute, 2006), 103.

15. Robert Putnam, *Bowling Alone: The Collapse and Revival of American Community* (New York: Simon and Schuster, 2002).

16. Gerald Monk et al, *Narrative Therapy in Practice: The Archaeology of Hope* (San Francisco: Jossey-Bass, 1997).

17. David Epston and Sallyann Roth, "Framework for a White/ Epston Type Interview" Watertown, MA: Family Institute of Cambridge, 1994).

18. Christie Neuger, *Counseling Women: A Narrative, Pastoral Approach* (Minneapolis: Augsburg Fortress, 2001); Archie Smith and Ursula Riedel-Pfaefflin, *Siblings by Choice: Race, Gender, and Violence* (St. Louis: Chalice Press, 2004).

19. Eric H. F. Law, *The Wolf Shall Dwell with the Lamb: A Spirituality for Leadership in a Multicultural Community* (St. Louis: Chalice Press, 1993), 76.

20. Appadurai, *Modernity at Large*.

21. H. Beecher Hicks, *On Jordan's Stormy Banks: Leading Your Congregation Through the Wilderness of Change* (Grand Rapids: Zondervan, 2004), 30.

22. Elizabeth P. Braxton, "God's Expansive Love" (sermon, Burke Presbyterian Church, Burke, VA, May 6, 2007).

23. Robert McKee, *Story: Substance, Structure, Style, and the Principles of Screenwriting* (New York: Regan Books, 1997).

24. Luther K. Snow, *The Power of Asset Mapping: How Your Congregation Can Act on Its Gifts* (Herndon, VA: Alban Institute, 2004); Mark Lau Branson, *Memories, Hopes, and Conversations: Appreciative Inquiry and Congregational Change* (Herndon, VA: Alban Institute, 2004); Susan Star Paddock, *Appreciative Inquiry in the Catholic Church* (Bend, OR: Thin Book Publishing, 2003); Gilbert R. Rendle and Alice Mann, *Holy Conversations: Strategic Planning as a Spiritual Practice for Congregations* (Herndon, VA: Alban Institute, 2003). See also Roy M. Oswald and Robert E. Friedrich, *Discerning Your Congregation's Future: A Strategic and Spiritual Approach* (Bethesda, MD: Alban Institute, 1996).

25. From Burke Presbyterian Church (BPC), Burke, PA, cottage meeting interview sheet, 2007.

26. Member quotes from interview responses recorded at each BPC cottage meeting.

27. Dietrich Bonhoeffer, *Life Together* and *Prayerbook of the Bible*, Dietrich Bonhoeffer Works, eds. Geffrey B. Kelly, Daniel W. Bloesch, James H. Burtness (Minneapolis: Fortress Press, 2004).

28. From Final Report of the BPC (Burke Presbyterian Church) Discernment Team, Burke, VA, June 2, 2007.

29. Butler Bass, *Christianity for the Rest of Us*, 11. See also Diana Butler Bass, *The Practicing Congregation: Imagining a New Old Church* (Herndon, VA: Alban Institute, 2004), and Diana Butler Bass and Joseph Stewart-Sicking, eds., *From Nomads to Pilgrims: Stories from Practicing Congregations* (Herndon, VA: Alban Institute, 2005).

30. Butler Bass, *Practicing Congregation*, 95.

31. Ibid., 98.

32. A method shared with the larger Anglican communion at the 1998 Lambeth Conference of the Anglican Church. See http://www.takomaparkpc.org/AfricanBibleStudy.html.

33. *A New Century, A New Calling*, Washington National Cathedral, 2007; http://www.cathedral.org/cathedral/pdfs/Vision2007.pdf.

CHAPTER 2

The Continuous Thread of Revelation

PASTORAL MEMOIRS AND THE NARRATIVE IMAGINATION

~

G. LEE RAMSEY JR.

The events in our lives happen in a sequence in time, but in their significance to ourselves they find their own order, a timetable not necessarily—perhaps not possibly chronological. The time as we know it subjectively is often the chronology that stories and novels follow: it is the continuous thread of revelation.

—Eudora Welty

I shall mount beyond this my power of memory, I shall mount beyond it, to come to You, O lovely Light. What have you to say to me?

—Saint Augustine

The impulse to write the pastoral memoir is akin to the impulse to write fiction—to tell a story. The best pastoral memoirs, whether ancient or contemporary, tell a similar story: a pastor (and writer) seeks through imagination and memory "the continuous thread of revelation," as Eudora Welty puts it. From Augustine's *Confessions* to Thomas Merton's *The Seven*

Storey Mountain to Heidi Neumark's more recent *Breathing Space*, we see the pattern. The pastor imaginatively and selectively narrates his or her memories of childhood, family, education, calling, and ministry to draw together the strands of a life. However frayed or knotted, when examined these strands reveal a continuous story of meaning. The pastor who tells the story stands at the center narrating the twists and turns of life. But because he or she is a pastor under divine orders, God and the church are also central characters in the story of the pastor's life.

Pastoral memoirs take various shapes. Not quite autobiography, in the strictest sense of the term, the pastoral memoir is more selective than comprehensive in its focus. The memoir takes us deeper into the writer's own emotions and search for meaning than the autobiography, which is usually more concerned with the facts of one's life. The writer of the pastoral memoir is much more interested in understanding faith, ministry, and self in relationship to others than in the historical data of his or her life. Some do move episodically through the life of the writer, then pause at moments of powerful epiphanies, such as Merton's well-known *The Seven Storey Mountain*. Others, such as Barbara Brown Taylor in *Leaving Church*, focus upon recent life chapters—a decision to leave parish ministry, for example—as key to current self-understanding. Some memoirs mine the rich, deep veins of congregational life within a single church to narrate theological and biblical understandings of Christian ministry, such as Heidi Neumark's *Breathing Space* or Richard Lischer's *Open Secrets*. Still other memoirs, like Kathleen Norris's *Dakota*, invite the reader to stroll through routine experiences with the writer that become occasions of revelation, especially in Norris's case, in relationship to geography and the cycle of the liturgical and natural seasons. In each of these instances, the writer undergoes a written soul searching, as Vivian Gornick says in *The Situation and Story*, "to know not only why one is speaking but *who* is speaking."[1] Whatever the shape of the story, the writer of the pastoral memoir seems to say, "Through these experiences of ministry and life, here is what I have learned of God, myself, and others."

Memoirs and Revelation

Theologically, the pastoral memoir stakes its claim in the territory of incarnation. The pastor tells her story to listeners because she believes that through the actual events of life and ministry, the incarnate God is speaking. To be sure, the writer checks her experience through theology, Scripture, and the witness of the church. Theological humility grounds the best pastoral memoirs. But the fact remains: the pastoral memoir invites us to consider human experience as a site of revelation.

This is what makes the well-written pastoral memoir so engaging. If the narrator (the writer) seems trustworthy, and if he tells his story in such a way that convinces us that his journey may lead us towards some form of wisdom, we will follow him into his remembered experiences.[2] Most significant, if Christ is speaking through the life of the pastor, we might want to know what he is hearing. The pastoral memoir allows us as readers to overhear the sounds of the gospel reverberating through the life of the minister. It clarifies or challenges our own reckonings of pastoral ministry and, whether or not we are ordained ministers, provides clues to where in our lives God may be found, or better yet, where God may find us. This is what makes the pastoral memoir so engaging.

Frederick Buechner puts it well in his memoir, *The Sacred Journey*: "Once I have put away my album for good, you may in the privacy of the heart take out the album of your own life and search it for the people and places you have loved and learned from yourself, and for those moments in the past—many of them half forgotten—through which you glimpsed, however dimly and fleetingly, the sacredness of your own journey."[3] Buechner's poetic invitation echoes Augustine's observation in the *Confessions* that memory is the vehicle, but the ultimate aim of the believer's remembrance is to ask God, "What have you to say to me?" The self-emptying God speaks or remains silent in many ways. One of those ways is through the flesh and blood of each of our lives recalled, rediscovered, renewed through memory.

Why Memoirs Matter

But, at the level of Christian practice, what do pastoral memoirs offer to the busy pastor and active layperson in Christian ministry? How can this particular expression of the narrative imagination—the pastoral memoir—inform the life and work of those who minister in the name of Jesus Christ? How does the pastoral memoir help shape the pastoral imagination as "a way of seeing into and interpreting the world?"[4] In what ways do the most recent pastoral memoirs help shape our own imaginations for Christian ministry, and in what ways are they a hindrance or an irrelevance? Are they simply interesting stories about someone else's ministry with little relevance to our own unique lives? Or does the pastoral memoir, like fine fiction, offer the promise of good stories well told—humanity with all its color and humor, depth and light, wisdom and companionship, and divinity that redeems the pasts and creates new worlds? Is it possible that the pastoral memoir can provide "strength for the journey," as Diana Butler Bass says of the Eucharist in her memoir?[5] In short, why bother reading the pastoral memoir anyway?

Clearing a Roadblock

We should begin by facing a potential roadblock—the writing. This may sound odd at first glance. But one hurdle the reader of the pastoral memoir must clear is the actual writing of the story. Not that these pastoral memoirs are poorly written. On the contrary, the best pastoral memoirs are usually well crafted, if not exquisitely so. The writers of these memoirs demonstrate gifted imaginations and writing skills. That's partly why their writing makes it into print. The prose of Frederick Buechner (*Sacred Journey; Now and Then*), Barbara Brown Taylor (*Leaving Church*), or Kathleen Norris (*Dakota*) hums like fine poetry. These writers love the beauty and know the power of words. As Norris says, "We [writers] are people who believe in the power of words to effect change in the human heart."[6] The language alone draws in many readers. Smart, sharp turns of phrase punctuate the writing styles of Richard Lischer (*Open Secrets*), Garret Keizer (*A Dresser of Sycamore Trees*), and Heidi Neumark (*Breathing Space*). For example, reflecting upon his mother's influence upon his call to ministry, Richard Lischer startlingly observes, "She never came out and admitted it, but I always suspected that she had cut some kind of deal with God along the lines of 'You give me a son, I'll give you a pastor.'"[7] Reading these memoirs, you can't help but admire the way the writers deftly handle language joined with insight. Therein lies the problem.

Many pastors are neither gifted poets nor accomplished writers. Most, we hope, do appreciate the wonder of words, since language is all wrapped up in creation and salvation. And ideally pastors are careful with the words they choose to communicate the good news of Jesus Christ through preaching and teaching. But this does not mean that every pastor is a

Shakespeare. Though unintended, the well-crafted prose of the pastoral memoir may keep the reader at a distance. He or she cannot accept the writer's invitation to join the story because the words are too lovely, the metaphors too apt, the writing too incisive. It can all seem a little too neat for the day-to-day pastor who has just returned from a head-butting committee meeting. When it arrives on the page, the memory and meaning of the writer seems so refined that the working pastor feels either slightly inferior or cannot fully trust the story as it unfolds. Either way, the pastoral memoir might fail to engage the imagination of the pastor who would otherwise welcome the story's insight in another form.

I don't know if much can be done about the problem, if it is a problem, except to caution and encourage. The pastor need not be an exquisite writer to appreciate the gifts of the well-written pastoral memoir. One should not feel intimidated by the beauty of these pastoral memoirs nor their insight, since some very few pastors, in my observation, actually have this remarkable gift (*charism*). Many pastors intuitively understand the ministry. Others approach it logically. Some are befuddled by the whole thing. And some, a very few, write about the ministry so well that it brings frequent nods of recognition and occasional tears to the eyes of those who read the accounts. If the writers take poetic license to tell the story of their lives artfully, why hold it against them? They are pointing us towards mystery and meaning within a vocation that depends upon both. For example, when the Lutheran Heidi Neumark tells of first lifting the lid of an unused baptismal font in a cavernous sanctuary in the South Bronx and says, "I lifted the lid to discover a film of dust and the remains of a few dead roaches. Paradise had become a desert, and I felt like I had stepped inside of Sarah's womb," we can take it as a too carefully wrought description of ministry that fails to connect with our experience. Or, we can receive it as a remarkably apt image of the barrenness that can overtake ministry.[8] In skillful, imaginative prose,

Neumark offers a vivid metaphor of ministry that links sense and sight, and says to us, the readers, "Here is what stagnation in ministry looks and feels like."

If such writing gets in the way of one's engagement in the ministry, then the pastoral memoir may not be the best genre to pursue. But for those who do find the genre appealing, with its unique narrative style that bends ministry experience towards artful representation, the memoir offers riches for the pastoral imagination.

Known by the Stories We Tell

Flannery O'Connor once commented on the difference between stories and statements of facts by saying, "In the long run, a people is known, not by its statements or its statistics, but by the stories it tells."[9] The pastoral memoir leans more towards story and narrative than documentation and facts. The writer of the pastoral memoir applies a narrative imagination to the experiences of ministry to tell a story that reveals not only the writer as person and pastor but also ministry as a storied world, richly populated by characters in the congregation who undergo conflicts in the community, theological and moral dilemmas, and unexpected twists and turns of plot. James Hopewell, an Episcopal priest and practical theologian, was one of the first to name the storied structure of congregational identity in his groundbreaking book *Congregation: Stories and Structures*.[10] Many, including those who write pastoral memoirs, have built upon his initial understandings of the narrative shape of congregations and ministry.

When we read Richard Lischer's *Open Secrets*, the story of his first three years in ministry among the people of New Cana, Illinois, we come away with an understanding of the real schooling of the young pastor, Lischer, at the hands of a

forgiving if obstinate congregation. But we also put down the
book with the voices of the members of New Cana Lutheran
congregation rattling around in our own heads. In telling us his
story within the congregation, Lischer can't help but tell the
congregation's story at the same time. They are known to us by
the stories he tells. And when he decides to leave for another
call, it is the elder Leonard Semanns who sums up the entwin-
ing of the congregational story with the pastor's story by saying, "Most us will stay right here, but wherever you go, you will
be carrying a little piece of Cana with you." By telling the story
in this particular way, Lischer has told us both who he is and
who the people of New Cana congregation are. It is no surprise
that Lischer summarizes at the end of his memoir, "I do make
sense of my life from that ministry."[11] A people is known, as
O'Connor says, "by the stories it tells."

Seizing the Narrative Imagination

Such creative renderings of ministry can enliven the imagination of the pastor and the layperson in various ways. While
very few of us can tell our stories as deftly as Nora Gallagher
(*Things Seen and Unseen; Practicing Resurrection*) or Barbara
Brown Taylor, or as insightfully as Richard Lischer, their gifts
can enrich our own. Their stories can amplify the ways we imagine ministry. Sifted through theology, Scripture, and church
tradition, their memories of ministry can help us to more fully
understand our own. Lending us their vision, perhaps we can
more fully see below the tedious surface of ministry into the
depths where shining insights flash and dart away into the future. Maybe we can come closer to saying what is true about
our own callings by listening to their voices.

So how can the working pastor cultivate an imagination
that helps him or her see ministry with greater creativity to

find "breathing space," to tell "open secrets," and to "practice resurrection"? If it is true, as Garrett Green says, that "to save sin-
ners, God seizes them by the imagination," how does the pastor
remain open to such "God-seizures" of the imagination?[12] Here
are several ways that the pastoral memoir can stir the narrative
imagination of the pastor.

Listening to Your Life

Toward the end of his memoir *Now and Then*, Presbyterian
minister and writer Frederick Buechner says, "Listen to your
life. See it for the fathomless mystery that it is. In the bore-
dom and pain of it no less than in the excitement and gladness:
touch, taste, smell your way to the holy and hidden heart of
it because in the last analysis all moments are key moments,
and life itself is grace."[13] Buechner invites and reminds us to see
grace in the comings and goings of our lives as pastors and as
laypeople. Something about ministry obscures vision, occludes
hearing. Pastors may slowly lose the ability to see the subtle
signs of God's presence in their own lives and in the lives of
those around them. Perhaps it is the relentless routine of a regular weekly cycle that dims the senses. Too many sermons, too
little time. Maybe it is the disheartening discovery that every
congregation has its naysayers, those who wouldn't believe God
is moving if the ark washed up on their doorsteps. Whatever
the cause, pastors can grow deaf to the sounds of grace—so
deaf they stop listening altogether. Here is where the memoir
provides aid.

The memoir enchants theologically; it helps us to "name
grace."[14] The pastoral memoir points us to where and how
grace appears in the life of the pastor. Like Barbara Brown Taylor, who thinks, upon hearing the honking sounds of wild geese
flying overhead, "I could not have asked for more blessed assur-
ance that my life had really changed."[15] Or, as Heidi Neumark
says, when seeing how the loving connection between a severely

burned father and his children gives the father hope to endure, "Connection is everything. Relationship to God and each other is life itself."[16] The grace that sustains ministry happens right where pastors and laity live. The pastoral memoir points us to the sacraments, to the rowdiest of church meetings, to the hospital room and the parking lot. All are sites of God's presence if we have eyes to see and ears to hear. Imagine that.

Discovering the Thread of Revelation

In Ralph Ellison's stunning yet incomplete novel, *Juneteenth*, the central character, the aging Rev. Alonzo Hickman, looks back over his life. Resisting the need for sleep, he says to himself, "You'll be asleep a long time and soon. Meanwhile, stay awake and watch the story unfold."[17] The pastoral memoir looks back at a season or lifetime of ministry and watches how the story unfolds. With a long backward look, the pastor takes her bearings for the present and future. This careful look at one's own story deepens the imagination of the pastor, especially the pastor who has been floating listlessly upon the surface of a ministry once flowing with life. The memoir can spark the imagination of the pastor by helping her discover Welty's "continuous thread of revelation" that courses through the forgotten and neglected channels of one's life. As Taylor recalls, after being pushed into a swimming pool full of other lost and found human beings, "Bobbing in that healing pool with all those other flawed beings of light, I looked around and saw them as I had never seen them before, while some of them looked at me the same way. The long wait had come to an end. I was in the water at last."[18] Through the imagination, the pastor sees her calling not so much as a lonely, sluggish drift through time but as a continuous, life-giving thread of meaning that joins her together with all the rest of humanity.

As the pastor scans whole chapters of ministry and life, redemptive themes emerge for both the minister and the

congregation. When we look back over ministry, we might begin to discover it as a "dressing of sycamore trees" (Keizer) or as
a "sacred journey" (Buechner). For Heidi Neumark, transfiguration (and the Church of the Transfiguration) gives way to
"breathing space" for all God's people. For Diana Butler Bass,
an Episcopal layperson and writer, Christian practices provide
"strength for the journey" of life and ministry. And for Richard
Lischer, the true secrets of ministry—the ones that should be
told—are heard among the rural people of Southern Illinois
who tell "open secrets" if the pastor is able to listen. As Garret
Keizer says, "I have tried to listen, as I believe Jesus did, for the
stories that can become parables."[19] Pastoral memoirs help us
imagine or reimagine our own ministry as story shaped, parable-like, and pregnant with meaning. Christian ministry is not
a random series of events that we tack upon the pegboard of
life or work. Ministry occurs within a story about God and us.
If we listen well to that story, we will hear the sounds of a continuous thread of revelation, like familiar voices drifting from a
darkened porch at nightfall.

Lives Narrated by Scripture

The turn to narrative has been one of the most fruitful avenues
in biblical study over the past forty years. The entire project
that informs this book draws from a wealth of narrative theory,
as outlined in Larry Golemon's introductory essay. Without
completely rejecting historical-critical approaches to Scripture,
many have begun to understand the biblical text as a living
story with God as the central character. As believers who live
(and die) by this story, the aim is to allow Scripture to "read us,"
to find where and how the Bible draws us into its story and in-
scribes our lives with gospel sense, usually understood in some
way as an alternative story to the dominant stories—economic, social, political—of contemporary culture. The approach
is appealing.

The problem is that many pastors and preachers don't quite know what to do with narrative, whether in preaching, spiritual direction, pastoral care, or administration. Some of us have been preaching *about* Scripture for so long and so unimaginatively that we no longer hear Scripture preaching about us. We approach the scriptural text as if it is an object to be dissected and explained rather than as a Spirit-moving story that invites us to walk around among its characters and scenes and find our surprising place.

Here the pastoral memoirs provide direction. Neumark's and Lischer's stories are especially helpful. Their memoirs show us pastors and congregations who allow themselves to *be* read by Scripture. For example, Neumark relates how the story of the widow of Zarephath (1 Kings 17) gave shape to the stories of single mothers within her own congregation— mothers struggling to find enough food to feed their children while remaining faithful.

> The official commentators call it the "Elijah cycle," but looking closer, I see it was the open hand of that widow in Zarephath that kept the cycle spinning. It's still spinning. I see it every day. The hands of those who continue to open out to others in spite of so many closed doors, in spite of drought and famine—these are the hands that nurture life and witness grace.
>
> One of the best examples is Burnice. When I met her, she was a single mother like the widow, facing life beside a dried-up brook. She dropped out of school as a teenager when her first baby came along. A series of men battered her heart and broke her bones, much as her alcoholic father had done . . . but Burnice has not closed her hands. . . . On Sundays Burnice stands before the altar holding out bread to share with all who come to receive it from her hands.[20]

From Zarephath to the South Bronx, Scripture weaves its world of meaning. The pastor, as Neumark says, is sometimes carried along reluctantly in the belly of a whale. But if she is willing to trust Scripture and the Spirit who breathes life upon it, she may find herself beached upon new, imaginative shores of pastoral and biblical understanding that will enrich her entire ministry.

Moving with the Seasons of the Gospel

Many of the writers of contemporary pastoral memoirs delight in the seasons of the Christian year. Nora Gallagher, an Episcopal lay minister and writer, structures her memoir, *Things Seen and Unseen,* around the entire Christian calendar, beginning with Advent and ending with Ordinary Time.[21] Similarly, Diana Butler Bass's *Strength for the Journey* gives sustained attention to the Christian seasons, especially worship services during the holy days of Lent and Easter. At one Easter vigil service at Christ Church in South Hamilton, Massachusetts, she sensed a "moment when the boundaries between heaven and earth thinned," where the congregation that gathered on Easter Eve knew themselves to "be God's pilgrim people, wanderers following God's way of justice."[22] Worship can do that. Following the liturgical calendar through the seasons of the gospel, worship draws us into the entire drama of salvation where we move with Christ and the historic church through birth, life, death, and resurrection.

Such liturgical immersion, so finely described in many of the pastoral memoirs, can deepen the narrative imagination of the pastor. This may be especially true for Protestant pastors who come from less liturgically oriented traditions, but it can also renew the imagination of all those pastors for whom the liturgical seasons have become repetitive and dull. The seasons of the Christian year and the particular biblical stories associated with them can soak the imaginations of pastors with symbols and images that flow refreshingly through their preaching, worship leadership, and Christian education. The challenge for pastors is to imaginatively locate themselves and the congregation within the larger story of God and to allow the seasons within that story to carry them along into the fullness of time.

Doing Justice, Loving Kindness

Imagination thieves stalk the halls of many churches. One of the most lethal of these bandits demands institutional maintenance so persistently that it leeches away the minister's passion for biblical justice. For many clergy, especially in mainline Protestant traditions, where middle- and upper-middle-class economic concerns predominate, God's desire for humanity voiced by the biblical prophet Micah—to do justice, love kindness, and walk humbly with God (6:8)—becomes almost inaudible amid the cacophonous (and frequently desperate) shouts to raise the budget and build more parking spaces. Whether the setting is a small church trying to stay alive or a large church trying to grow bigger, a lot of time and money is spent on physical plants and bottom lines, while the imagination for ministry is held hostage. Meanwhile, the poor continue to work for less than a living wage, if they work at all, and those without any health care multiply daily. All this happens in a country that spends billions of dollars a day to fund an ill-advised war in a country torn apart by civil strife. Yet the church's call for biblical justice is muted throughout the land. It is almost enough to make the downhearted pastor agree with the iconoclastic Will Campbell when he says, especially with the church in mind, "All institutions, and I mean *all* of 'em, are fundamentally inimical to what Christ was about on this earth."[23]

Yet allowing oneself to be robbed of hope, conceding to despair, has always been one of the greatest temptations of the faithful. What is needed is a new imagination, a renewal of the mind (Rom. 12:2) that helps the pastor and congregation see their mission in a new light. Here, surprisingly, the pastoral memoir can help.

There is no telling how many times Dorothy Day's plainly written memoir *The Long Loneliness* has strengthened hope and passion for biblical justice. Henri Nouwen's confession-like journals of his sojourns in Latin America (*Gracias!*) and his reflections upon servant leadership among the L'Arche community in Toronto (*In the Name of Jesus*) have helped ground many Christians in practices that wed justice with mercy.[24]

We discover similar sources for renewal in the pastoral memoirs of Neumark and Keizer. These memoirs are not so much exercises in personal introspection as they are reflections upon the challenges of living out a faithful ministry amid the complexities and injustices of the late twentieth and early twenty-first centuries, whether in rural Vermont or the bustling Bronx. They do not offer a prescription for how pastors and congregations can remain focused upon mission and worship, but they do provide moving accounts of how their particular congregations have attempted to do so. When hearing one of Neumark's many stories about how she and her congregation began to take the ministry of Transfiguration into the rough-and-tumble streets of the South Bronx, if we listen carefully we can hear a gentle summons saying, "So what would that look like around our church? Who needs Holy Communion outside the walls of this building, and how do we come along beside them?" That is how imagination works. That is how the streams of new life start flowing.

Listen to Garret Keizer describe the ministry of another priest, Jeannette McKnight, whose commitment to kindness and justice sends jolts of awareness through his own imagination:

> As neat and proper as a hat on a schoolmarm's head, extremely methodical, Jeannette McKnight [is] ... [an] extremely unaffected feminist, she refuses to call any priest "Father," after Jesus' injunction, or to let anyone call her "Mother." Yet she wears a dress whenever she wears her clerical collar to avoid

"threatening" those as yet unadjusted to a woman in a traditional man's role. Her local reputation for quiet courage is
perhaps the best-kept secret in our diocese. She offers sanctuary to battered women, disarms their pistol-toting husbands,
presents seminars on gay awareness—in Lyndonville, Vermont—then walks briskly home to make lunch for herself
and her husband or to catch up on her sewing. She kills me.[25]

Pastors don't need to meet Jeannette McKnight in person.
Garret Keizer has already introduced us to her in a way that
sets spinning the wheels of the imagination. We need not remain victims of institutional drag. We have stories and companions like Jeannette McKnight to help us do justice, love
kindness, and walk humbly with God. This leads to one final
contribution that the pastoral memoir makes to the narrative
imagination of the pastor.

Imaginative Companions

Dorothy Day concludes *The Long Loneliness* by saying, "We
have all known the long loneliness and we have learned that the
only solution is love and that love comes with community. It all
happened while we sat there talking, and it is still going on." It
is a lovely image of community. Christ breaks and redeems the
long loneliness of ministry by the gift of human community
in which "we know Him in the breaking of the bread, and we
know each other . . . and we are not alone any more."[26]

The last and best gift of the pastoral memoir may be companions in ministry who stir our own imaginations. Reading
the memoir, we see the kind of human community that nurtures and challenges the writer. These pastoral memoirs are
not about isolated clergy but about pastors who are called and
shaped by particular communities—like the congregation of

Grace-Calvary Episcopal Church in Clarksville, Georgia, welcoming their new rector, Barbara Brown Taylor, by giving her
and her husband two rocking chairs. "I was being invited to
sit down and stay a while, which I fully intended to do," says
Taylor.[27] Or like Richard Lischer being told by one of the Lutheran elders during his first meeting with the New Cana, Illinois, congregation, "I didn't vote for you, but I know we will
have a very good church with you as our pastor."[28] Now that
either pushes the pastor toward genuine community or sends
him running in the other direction.

Real communities are populated by real characters who accompany the pastor in ministry—characters like the elderly
Jeffrey in Keizer's *Dresser of Sycamore Trees*, who has cerebral
palsy. He says to the unsuspecting Keizer, "If I were cured to-
morrow at seven-fifteen, it would be the greatest tragedy of
my life. Because knowing my weakness, I know I would forget
about God by four."[29] Or characters like Dodie Little of Trinity
Church in Santa Barbara, California, who says to Diana Butler Bass that Trinity was transformed because "we were forced
to look at each other, and we really *saw* each other for the
first time."[30]

These are the types of characters who walk beside pastors
in congregations. They can be found in every sanctuary and fel-
lowship hall where Christians gather. Ministry does not occur
in solitude, though solitude can certainly nourish the spiritual
and emotional life of the pastor. Ministry occurs among the
characters whom pastors know as the people of God, the communion of saints. The way the pastoral memoir presents them
helps pastors imagine the characters of their own congregations as part of the cast of a much larger divine drama, with
each character playing his or her part. The imaginative companions of the memoir give way to the true companions who
surround pastors in ministry. With them pastors can converse,
argue, disagree, pray, and forgive. Together, in true community,
all seek to love and serve the risen Lord.

God's Continuous Thread

Who can say, in the end, what will seize the narrative imagination of the pastor, the student of ministry, or the Christian
layperson? Some folks seem to effortlessly spin, carousel-like,
upon colorful, lovely, even zany imaginations. They see and
hear stories everywhere that tell of a bread-breaking Savior
and a pilgrim people. They need little encouragement to create
image and story and link them to a lively ministry. For others, the characters within Scripture and tradition seem distant
from the people in the pew. They struggle to connect the tena-
cious widow of Zarephath with an almost spent but still trusting congregation. A ministry enriched by narrative imagination
does not quite fit. Finding the connections is hard.

For either type of leader, or others who fall somewhere between, the pastoral memoir offers direction. But for all types
of leaders in all situations, the pastoral memoir can offer direction. If the narrative imagination is sluggish, the pastoral
memoir pumps new zest into ministry. It can help clergy and
laity see and hear fresh stories of other congregations that are
realistically imaginable. The characters of Lischer's or Neumark's memoirs, for example, can "in-spire" (breathe spirit
into) the minister and the congregation. On the other hand,
if the narrative imagination is already revved up, the memoir
can provide additional spark for the race of faith. It offers en-
ergized companions and parable-like stories to accompany us
along the way.

Either way, the pastoral memoirs available today show and
tell how the stories, characters, and settings of ministry all work
together—if we watch them closely—to reveal the continuous
thread of revelation. If, in a day where it sometimes seems the
louder we shout the less God is heard, the pastoral memoir
stirs our imagination enough so that we steadily perceive the
tracings of God within ministry, that would be gift enough.

Notes

~

Eudora Welty, *One Writer's Beginnings* (Cambridge, MA: Harvard University Press, 1983), 68–69; and *The Confessions of St. Augustine*, Books 1–9, trans. F. J. Sheed (Kansas City, MO: Sheed and Ward, 1942), 186.

1. Vivian Gornick, *The Situation and the Story: The Art of Personal Narrative* (New York: Farrar, Straus and Giroux, 2001), 8.

2. Ibid., 14.

3. Frederick Buechner, *The Sacred Journey: A Memoir of Earlier Days* (San Francisco: Harper & Row, 1982), 7.

4. C. R. Dykstra, "The Pastoral Imagination," *Initiatives in Religion* 9 (2001): 2–3, 15.

5. Diana Butler Bass, *Strength for the Journey: A Pilgrimage of Faith in Community* (San Francisco: Jossey-Bass, 2002).

6. Kathleen Norris, *Dakota: A Spiritual Geography* (Boston: Houghton Mifflin, 1993), 105.

7. Richard Lischer, *Open Secrets: A Memoir of Faith and Discovery* (New York: Broadway Books, 2001), 20.

8. Heidi B. Neumark, *Breathing Space: A Spiritual Journey in the South Bronx* (Boston: Beacon Press, 2003), 10.

9. Flannery O'Connor, *Mystery and Manners: Occasional Prose*, ed. Sally and Robert Fitzgerald (New York: Farrar, Straus and Giroux, 1993), 192.

10. James F. Hopewell, *Congregation: Stories and Structures*, ed. Barbara G. Wheeler (Philadelphia: Fortress Press, 1987).

11. Lischer, *Open Secrets*, 236, 238.

12. Garrett Green, *Imagining God: Theology and the Religious Imagination* (San Francisco: Harper & Row, 1989), 149.

13. Frederick Buechner, *Now and Then: A Memoir of Vocation* (New York: Harper & Row, 1983), 87.

14. See Mary Catherine Hilkert, *Naming Grace: Preaching and the Sacramental Imagination* (New York: Continuum, 1997), for an excellent exploration of the sacramental imagination and ministry.

15. Barbara Brown Taylor, *Leaving Church: A Memoir of Faith* (San Francisco: HarperSanFrancisco, 2006), 63.

16. Neumark, *Breathing Space*, xvii.

17. Ralph Ellison, *Juneteenth*, ed. John F. Callahan (New York: Random House, 1999), 275.

18. Taylor, *Leaving Church*, 120.

19. Garret Keizer, *A Dresser of Sycamore Trees: The Finding of a Ministry* (San Francisco: HarperSanFrancisco, 1991), 50.

20. Neumark, *Breathing Space*, 46–49.

21. Nora Gallagher, *Things Seen and Unseen: A Year Lived in Faith* (New York: Vintage Books, 1998).

22. Bass, *Strength for the Journey*, 79

23. Will Campbell, in Marshall Frady, *Southerners: A Journalist's Odyssey* (New York: New American Library, 1980), 373.

24. Dorothy Day, *The Long Loneliness: An Autobiography* (San Francisco: Harper & Row, 1952); Henri J. M. Nouwen, *Gracias! A Latin American Journal* (San Francisco: Harper & Row, 1983); Nouwen, *In the Name of Jesus: Reflections on Christian Leadership* (New York: Crossroad, 1997).

25. Keizer, *Dresser of Sycamore Trees*, 69–70.

26. Day, *Long Loneliness*, 285–86.

27. Taylor, *Leaving Church*, 90.

28. Lischer, *Open Secrets*, 43.

29. Keizer, *Dresser of Sycamore Trees*, 10.

30. Bass, *Strength for the Journey*, 202.

CHAPTER 3

Pastor as Narrative Leader

~

N. GRAHAM STANDISH

When I came to Calvin Presbyterian Church in Zelieno-ple in 1996 to be its pastor, I came as a misfit. I wasn't a social misfit as much as I was a religious misfit. I just didn't seem to fit very well into the dominant, mainline Protestant religious culture of the mid-1990s. Whatever the dominant ministry model of the time was, it wasn't one that spoke to me or my experience.

At the time, I was relatively young (in my mid-thirties) during a time in which all the churches of our denomination seemed to be looking for pastors with long-term experience. The reigning wisdom was that only a pastor with exten-sive ministry background could stem the tide of losses most churches were experiencing at the time. It didn't matter that the experience many of those pastors had was in leading declin-ing churches. The belief was that younger pastors just didn't have enough practice and, therefore, skill to right the listing ships that were the mainline congregations of the 1990s. So, I was also an *age* misfit. I was a young pastor in a denomination looking for older ones.

At the same time, my main interest was in the area of spiri-tuality. I had devoted a significant portion of the previous eight years reading, studying, and practicing the wisdom of Christian spiritual writers throughout the ages. It all culminated in my getting a PhD in spiritual formation in 1995. I was a misfit at the time because mainline Protestantism was still caught in the throes of an emphasis on tradition and theological thinking. That has changed in recent years as more and more church leaders recognize both the need for an emphasis on spirituality in churches and seminaries and the emergence of a spiritual thirst among people in North American culture. Still, I was a *spiritual* misfit in a theologically focused denomination.

I also had a vision for church that contrasted both with the mainline traditions and with the growing evangelical, contemporary movement. My vision was of a church that would seek spiritual growth over numerical growth, one that emphasized creating a community of faith that might well remain somewhat small. I also had a vision for a congregation that would attract people who felt like misfits, people who didn't necessarily feel like they fit into the typical church crowd. They would be people who wanted to grow spiritually, but who felt like they didn't fit in the more traditional or contemporary ways of doing church. I realize now that my vision was very similar to what is today called the emergent church movement, but the term *emergent* wouldn't be coined for another seven years.

When I came to Calvin Church in 1996, it became apparent to me that I was a misfit pastor leading a misfit church. I don't know that the members of Calvin Church necessarily like it when I say that we are a misfit church. Most of the congregation's members don't feel like misfits, at least not socially, but they are misfits in a spiritual sense. Calvin Church is a moderate Presbyterian church with an emphasis on spiritual growth through prayer and discernment in an area dominated by traditional, conservative churches and new contemporary evangelical churches. What has become clearly evident to me over time is that in many ways my story and Calvin Church's story parallel each other.

Four families of Scottish descent founded Calvin Presbyterian Church in 1845. The Zelienople area was settled several decades before by German immigrants. Many were Lutheran, some were German Reformed, and some were part of a relatively obscure Anabaptist sect called the Harmonites. These four Scottish families were religious misfits. The churches of the area conducted their services primarily in German. As a result, these four families didn't quite fit religiously and spiritually into this culture. So they decided to start a congregation for people like them: folks who were committed to living in the area, but who wanted to find a place where they could worship in the Scottish Reformed ways.

The congregation thrived for its first fifty years, growing in faith, membership, and size. They were a church of misfits who reached out to other misfits. The church started to struggle a bit as it became a different congregation in the early parts of the twentieth century. As the century progressed, it became known as a church for wealthy people, although that is a relative term since the Zelienople and Harmony areas hardly became bastions of great wealth. The church held its membership steady throughout the twentieth century, but began to decline during the 1970s, '80s and '90s as internal congregational conflicts collided with cultural trends that caused many in the U.S. population to decide that Christianity no longer had relevance.

Reflecting on my coming to Calvin Church, I realize now that my story and the congregation's story were congruent. I have always been something of a religious misfit because of my perceptions and interests, and Calvin Church has mostly been a church that attracted those who felt as though they have not fit in to the local religious culture.

Looking at my story and Calvin Presbyterian Church's respective stories, it is apparent that in many ways we dovetail and are living the same story. Of course, I am not the only pastor who is living according to a plotline that intersects Calvin Church's story. Nor is the story I have just articulated the only story that can be told about Calvin Church. There are numerous other possible narratives. For instance, Calvin Church was a mission church in many ways in its beginning. A pastor with a passion for mission could do wonders in articulating that aspect of Calvin's story. Another pastor with an interest in creating a community church could also tease out that aspect of Calvin Church's story. What I have managed to do as the pastoral leader of Calvin Church is to find a way to meld my story and the congregation's story so that together we are writing new chapters that fit with the overall plot and theme of a story that has already been unfolding.

While many pastors' stories would mesh with Calvin's, many pastors have stories that would not mesh, and they would have difficulty leading the congregation in a positive direction. Why? Because they would have to actually stop the processes of the church's ongoing story and try to rewrite a whole new plotline. For instance, if a Pentecostal-style pastor became the pastor of Calvin Church, emphasizing the need to speak in tongues and save souls, she would quickly become embroiled in controversy. This approach to Christian faith has never been part of Calvin Church's story. It would create a clash of story lines that would leave the church adrift in confusion as people competed to write the next chapter of the church's story or fought to return the church to its original plotline. A congregation's story must have some consonance with its pastoral leader's story if it is to thrive. How the pastor engages his story with the church's story is also crucial to whether or not he leads the church in a healthy direction.

The Centrality of Story to Human Life

To what extent do congregational leaders value the importance of story in leadership? Our congregations exist in an age of science, technology, and rational thought. This age, at least from the scientific perspective, treats story, mythology, drama, and literature as secondary human endeavors—second to logical, rational, sequential thought. In many ways, ours is a rational, logical culture that praises seemingly objective, discursive, and analytical approaches to thinking through problems and situations to find answers and solutions. Throughout the twentieth century, the dominant leadership strategy distilled organizational management to objectively defined criteria with a belief that if the right, properly tested techniques were used by a leader, the organization would thrive. In many ways, this method developed out of the assembly-line approaches to everything that emerged from the industrial revolution.

As a result of the dominance of scientific, rational, logical strategy to leadership, and also to politics, economics, psychology, business, medicine, and much more, the value of story, myth, legend, drama, and literature had become diminished by the late twentieth century. In ancient times, stories were considered to be vital vehicles that held wisdom, guidance, and God's voice. Today, people are more likely to think of stories as entertainment. We tend to dismiss mythology as ancient tales told by ignorant people who created stories to explain the mysteries of life, mysteries that made them scared and superstitious and that only science would later explain. We consider drama to be mainly for amusement, and often consider reading literature as an exercise for elitist intellectuals or for those with time on their hands.

Unfortunately, this scientific and positivistic view of human thinking ignores the reality of how humans think and understand life. We don't just learn and process thoughts through logic and rationality. We also have a natural tendency to grasp life through story, narrative. Humans are hardwired for it. Business researcher Daniel Pink, in his book *A Whole New Mind: Why Right-Brainers Will Rule the Future*, says that the emphasis on logic and rationality runs counter to how human brains actually work.[1] He says that we are not built for facts. Instead, we are hardwired for telling and remembering stories. Telling stories actually helps us assimilate facts and data by integrating the left and the right hemispheres of the brain. To understand the differences of the hemispheres, Pink says that the "left hemisphere reasoned sequentially, excelled at analysis, and handled words. The right hemisphere reasoned holistically, recognized patterns, and interpreted emotions and nonverbal expressions."[2] Normal human thinking brings the processes of our two brain hemispheres together in a way that brings us a more whole-brained awareness. Thus, story is essential to human understanding, for as cognitive scientist Don Norman says, "Stories have the felicitous capacity of capturing exactly those elements that formal decision making leave out. Logic tries to generalize, to strip the decision making from the specific context, to remove it from subjective emotions. Stories capture the context, capture the emotions. . . . Stories are important cognitive events, for they encapsulate, into one compact package, information, knowledge, context, and emotion."[3]

Human beings think in story. We learn through story. Reflect on this for a bit. When you were in school, when were you most likely to listen to the teacher? When giving a sequential, logical lecture, or when the teacher started telling stories? We might not have been able to recite all the points of a story, but we learned from them. It required much more work to memorize and digest facts. If we look at life honestly, we discover that our lives are filled with story. Spiritual books are filled with stories. Read any spiritual book, and you will find a book filled with stories. The Bible is filled with stories that have nurtured people for centuries. U.S. history is a story (often a story about overcoming crisis and conflict), and U.S. citizens know these stories well: the story of the Declaration of Independence, the Revolutionary War, the Civil War, the "taming" of the West, World War I, the Great Depression, World War II, the civil rights movement, the Vietnam War, and so forth. History is best told in stories, which makes sense since the two words have the same root. And individuals tell stories. We gather with our friends and tell story after story after story. Our stories tell others what we think, what our values are, and what we believe is important in life.

Unfortunately, when we dismiss something as being mere "myth," we ignore how powerful a force in human life myths can be. Myth isn't a collection of stories by ignorant, ancient people. Myth is the primary vehicle we use to reveal spiritual truth that cannot be accessed through anything other than metaphor. As Bill Moyers defined it, in his conversations with the great mythology scholar, Joseph Campbell, "Myths are stories of our search through the ages for truth, for meaning, for significance," to which Campbell replied, "Myth helps you to put your mind in touch with this experience of being alive. It tells you what the experience is."[4]

Humans are living stories of experience. Our lives can be scripted like a narrative. In fact, when we think of individual lives in this way, what we discover is that those who live what seem to be successful lives have a generally compelling life narrative of overcoming obstacles in order to achieve. Those who seem to have dysfunctional lives often have life stories that read like disconnected or stuck narratives in which the main character struggles to overcome obstacles. Instead of overcoming obstacles, these obstacles overwhelm her or his life. Understanding the role of story is crucial to understanding the role narrative plays in leadership.

Leadership as Crafting a Story

Over the years I have noticed a definite difference between good leaders and great leaders, a difference that is more than just a matter of great leaders doing certain things *better* than good leaders. Good leaders lead people toward a goal. They are able to articulate a common aim for an organization, a department, a team, or a congregation. They are able to get people on board enough so that the goals become common goals. And these good leaders are able to motivate people to want to achieve these goals. This is all good stuff.

What seems to make great leaders great is not that they are better at envisioning and articulating goals, as well as being better at uniting and motivating people to achieve these goals. What I notice is that great leaders don't even talk so much in terms of goals and aims. Instead, great leaders seem to craft a story, a story that inspires others in the organization, team, or congregation so that they willingly become a part of and live out this story in their work and lives. Great leaders, through their whole style of leadership, tell a story about the organization or congregation that becomes a blueprint for its ongoing growth.

Does what I am saying seem like semantics? It isn't. Great leaders seem to understand intuitively that they are living out a story, and a compelling one at that, and they make sure that all the characters, no matter how quirky, fit together to move along a healthy narrative path. If they refuse to fit with the plot, they are removed. For instance, you see this difference in athletics between good coaches and great coaches. Good coaches prepare their players to play well in all circumstances. When the players don't play well, good coaches school them in the fundamentals so that they can play better. They hope that by preparing the team, the team can avoid insurmountable problems. The struggle comes when teams begin to suffer problems for which there are no answers. The good coaches don't know what to do to overcome the problems. Often they sit perplexed, trying to find a way to convince the players to play harder.

Great coaches seem to have a whole different understanding of what the team is doing. They prepare the players just like good coaches. They ensure that their teams are as fundamentally sound as possible. But they don't prepare the team to avoid insurmountable problems. They actually prepare the team with the expectation that these troubles will come, and that part of achieving success means overcoming these troubles. Great coaches embrace trouble and turmoil, with an understanding that unless the team encounters severe troubles, they will not be able to fulfill the essential plot: this team will overcome all troubles to eventually rise to the top and become victorious. In their embrace of impending hardship, they craft a story line that follows almost all great literary stories: The heroes face a challenge. They start out doing okay, but then they falter. They struggle in the face of unexpected disasters, disruptions, or disturbances. It looks like they might succumb to the pressures of their situations. But they then rise up and find a way to overcome the obstacles, bringing about some sort of redemption. In the end, they are able to overcome their troubles and achieve some sort of victory. It is a compelling story.

This theme of turning turmoil into triumph is played out constantly in literature and life. It could apply to a championship football team, a woman getting out of an abusive situation, a country fighting a war, a family struggling to get out of crushing poverty, or a village struggling through a drought. Great leaders seem to inherently understand these plotlines and are able to see difficulties and challenges as the natural obstacles an organization must face in order to rise above it.

I think about great leaders throughout history, and I see the story above reflected in their lives and leadership. As general of the colonial army, George Washington led the soldiers through defeats and retreats and helped them become stronger through them so that they were able to eventually defeat the mighty British army at Yorktown. Abraham Lincoln led the Union in the fight against the Confederates and faced the prospect of being beaten badly as Confederate troops came close to capturing Washington, D.C. But he persevered and overcame seemingly certain destruction to defeat the Confederates and restore unity to the United States of America. Mahatma Gandhi led the Indian people through the darkness of British occupation, but he never saw the beatings and imprisonments he and they suffered as insurmountable. He inherently saw them as difficulties that challenged the Indian people to become more resolute and united against the British. Jesus's story also follows this theme.

He led his disciples to great heights, only to be killed on the cross as his followers scattered. Yet he overcame the greatest obstacle of all: death. And in doing so he allowed the world to discover a greater way of living.

Great pastors tell a story through the churches they lead. They don't just create the conditions for a healthy congregation. They craft a story that allows the church to overcome situations that might crush a less resilient church. While they don't court trouble, they recognize that trouble may and will come to the church. As a pastor friend said to me many years ago, "It's when everything is going right in the church that I get worried, because I know something's coming." He didn't fear what was coming, but he understood that as a pastoral leader his role was to be ready for those times and to lead the congregation to overcome them. At the same time, the danger in thinking this way is that it can create a plotline in which good times are ignored as the leader scans the horizon for the eventual turmoil. But that was not his point. His point was that trouble comes. How people overcome it becomes the story.

You can hear how important this plotline is to great leaders. As they tell the story of their organization, they often cite how they overcame problems and challenges that might crush another company. They overcome these odds through a variety of strategies, but overcoming them is a crucial part of the story.

Let me share an example with you that comes from one of my favorite companies, Apple, Inc. (I am writing this on a Mac computer while listening to my iPod.) *Time* magazine did a profile of Apple in 2005, focusing on the story of how its founder, Steve Jobs, helped Apple overcome some very lean years in order to become what it is today, a company that offers a wide array of technology: computers, MP3 players, cell phones, and more.

The company was founded in 1976 by three men: Steve Jobs, Steve Wozniak, and Ronald Wayne (Wayne sold his interest in the company a year later). The company struggled for a few years, but by 1984 its personal computers, designed more for personal use than for business, had created a reputation for being innovative. Unlike other computer-oriented companies such as Microsoft, which focused on software, and IBM, which focused on hardware, Apple offered the whole package. For a number of years, spurred by sales of its Macintosh computer, Apple gained popularity for its design, especially for its desktop look that emphasized using a mouse to point and click, rather then the DOS command system most software programs were using.

Then in 1985 an internal power struggle developed within the company, and Steve Jobs, the CEO, was pushed out. In other words, conflict had created an obstacle, and Apple's response was to fire its founder and head. For a while the company thrived and succeeded without the headstrong Jobs, introducing products such as the first PowerBook, an easy to use, more ergonomically designed laptop computer. Then the company started to founder. It tried, under its new CEO, John Scully, to introduce new cutting-edge products, but the market just didn't seem to care for Apple products. They were confusing, poorly designed, and just as poorly marketed. Apple began a precipitous decline. With Microsoft now offering its new line of Windows software, software that used mice to click and point, the lead Apple had created in the market by offering a visual-based operating system vanished. Apple's decline seemed unstoppable as a series of CEOs replaced Scully.

This was the classic story of a successful company that couldn't write new chapters to its narrative. Apple was stuck in a plotline that seemed destined to end in disappointment and disillusionment. No matter who was hired as CEO, the company's plot seemed fixed and unalterable. The CEOs and the company would try to offer new products as an answer to their woes, but their narrative had become conventional to the point at which, not knowing what else to do, they began to lay off workers. Their focus was now as much on saving money as it was on increasing market share.

In 1996 the then-CEO, Gil Amelio, brought Steve Jobs back into the company as an adviser. In 1997, after Apple had experienced its worst three years since its inception, it replaced Amelio with Steve Jobs. From there the narrative changed from one of unalterable decline to one of overcoming obstacles in order to achieve great success.

One of the talents of great narrative leaders is that they see plotlines and possibilities that others do not. Their imagination is such that they can think outside of the normal narrative box—the narrative that is always stuck in conventional thinking. Jobs started changing the story by leading the company to take several bold steps, which brought about a transformation from conventional to potential thinking. The potential he saw lay in seeking avenues for Apple to become more accessible.

First, Apple signed an agreement with archrival Microsoft to allow Microsoft Office, its word processing, e-mail, and spreadsheet software programs, to be used on Apple products. This meant that Apple owners could finally use the same software as most other computer users. Then Jobs guided the company to open a series of Apple Stores that emphasized excellent service and flexibility of products. Then, with the help of designer Jonathan Ive (who later helped design the iPhone), Apple introduced a revolutionary computer, the iMac, which changed the design of computers to be elegant and exciting rather than simply functional and bland. Apple developed products for those who wanted to do more than word processing and spreadsheets on their computer, creating programs such as iMovie, which allowed anyone to create movies on their computers, and GarageBand, which allowed users to record and mix music on their computers. These were just a few of the many innovative changes that Jobs initiated.

What Jobs did next really changed the whole company. He envisioned Apple's transformation from a computer company to an entertainment company, and so in 2001 the first iPod was introduced, a digital audio player that was both functional and elegant. Along with it, Apple introduced iTunes, a software program that made the purchasing, downloading, and syncing between the computer and the iPod effortless. From there, Jobs has led Apple to introduce the iPhone and Apple TV.

Jobs looked at the obstacles and overcame them by seeing new and different plot possibilities. He envisioned a new narrative, and in the process transformed the story of Apple.[5]

The end of this story is that Jobs and Apple overcame doubters, as well as those wedded to conventional ways, to create a company that is generating new markets for itself. It refused to be *just* a computer company or *just* a software company. What Jobs has done as leader of Apple is to craft a narrative for Apple. He founded the company with that narrative. In the early 1990s he was let go of as chairman, and the company foundered. But then he was brought back. Armed with greater wisdom, but the same narrative, he has turned a small company into an ever-growing company that surprises people with its design and innovation.

While this is an example of leadership in a business organization, the principles are the same for congregations. Great pastoral leaders don't shy from conflict, problems, and difficulties. They understand that these are inevitable in church communities. What they are able to do is to face these challenges and lead a congregation to overcome them. To understand how, it is helpful to look at the elements of narrative leadership and then to reflect on how these elements relate to the telling of a compelling story.

Elements of Narrative Leadership

In doing research on understanding the structure of how compelling stories work in novels and films, I have been fascinated with how the best stories always follow a particular pattern of introduction, setup, crisis, transformation, redemption, and reformation. Whenever you have seen a film, a play, or a television show that has touched you deeply, or left you wanting to see it again, you have been part of a narrative that effectively uses the elements of the pattern above. Effective stories lead people through these elements in compelling ways. Great pastoral leaders also move their congregations through these elements. In contrast, ineffective leaders seem to be like authors stuck in writer's block or immersed in writing cliched, redundant story lines. Either they can't quite seem to find an alternative story line for the congregation and so get trapped in a crisis that seems to have no resolution, or they lead in a safe, bland way that not only protects them from crisis but also prevents an eventual transformation of both the congregation and the members.

Effective leaders creatively script their congregations' stories by finding alternative plotlines that lead to resolving the crises in a way that steers people to experience redemption, reconciliation, and sometimes resurrection. Great congregational leaders lead congregations, in some small way, to experience the Christian story of doing ministry, encountering crisis, experiencing suffering, undergoing death (of some sort), being resurrected, and achieving reconciliation.

Robert McKee, who is known as the scriptwriters' guru because so many Academy Award-nominated and winning directors, producers, and screenwriters have taken his workshops and applied his principles to their work, offers a great way of understanding the underlying structure of narrative leadership. His workshops and his book, *Story*, focus on the principles of storytelling.[6] By examining the principles of good storytelling as he presents them, one can gain insight into the structure of good narrative leadership. Many of the narrative principles presented by McKee are similarly reflected in the work of effective leaders and their congregations and organizations. McKee points out the narrative principles involved in three areas: story, structure, and transformation.

Story

The foundational principle of any effective narrative is story. In essence, good stories always reflect a clearly defined plot that follows the patterns of great drama throughout history. As McKee says, there are no new stories. Instead, modern drama reflects the story lines of great literature throughout history, which includes biblical literature. What makes these story lines so effective is that they reflect the basic themes of human living that were true in ancient times and still are true today. New stories do not present something entirely new. Instead, they reveal these traditional human themes in creative new ways.[7]

This principle of recapturing ancient themes in contemporary stories is especially true of drama that follows the principles of "archplot," the kind of plot that most of us typically gravitate toward in movies and novels. In archplot, characters are introduced to the reader or the viewer and encounter some conflicted situation that challenges them. The challenges, whatever they are, lead the main character into crisis, and that crisis leads to transformation.[8] The crisis must be resolved either through the main character transforming the circumstances (for example, leading the townspeople to lay down sandbags to save the local library) or through the main character becoming transformed as she overcomes the situation. The transformation eventually leads to the resolution of the conflict and to redemption of either the circumstances or the main character. For an example of exterior transformation, think of the film *Gladiator* in which the enslaved general transforms Rome in the end. For an example of interior transformation, think *Thelma and Louise* in which the women quit being victims and become self-confident. Films like the *Star Wars* and *The Lord of the Rings* have both interior and exterior transformation.

Similar kinds of transformations take place in congregational leadership. For instance, when I first came to Calvin Presbyterian Church, it had been a church in the midst of a thirty-year decline. Prior to my arrival, I had undergone a tremendous amount of personal transformation through my studies in psychology and spirituality, and also because of some very difficult personal experiences. I came to the congregation recognizing the need to lead it into transformation. My first few years at Calvin Church were a time of challenge in which I was bringing new ideas. I was met with some resistance (fortunately, not of epic proportions). The challenge was to overcome potential conflict—conflict with a church secretary who did not want to do the work that a growing church would bring; members who had personal issues with others in the church and wanted the drama program curtailed or gotten rid of; conflict with elders who did not particularly welcome a new focus on prayer and spirituality.

As a leader, I sought ways to overcome a plotline of decline and to lead the congregation to one of transformation and resurrection. In the process, I was always seeking to guide the church to a new story line: accomplishing what previously hadn't seemed possible by overcoming whatever obstacles stood in our way, such as a history of decline, a building in need of renovation, a reputation among the other churches in town as the church of "those" people. I was trying to rescript the previous plot that said, "We are a church in decline" into an alternative plot that said, "We can become a model for other churches to follow." Looking back, I had that script in my mind from the beginning, although I was only marginally aware of it. The congregation seemed to have been stuck in something akin to writer's block, and my role was to help script a new plotline that would lead to a different kind of resolution.

Just as all movies and novels in some way or another follow the plotlines of classic literature, I believe that healthy churches generally follow biblical story lines. For example, the plot of the Gospels is that despite Jesus's teachings of God's love and presence, angry skeptics in his midst wanted to do away with him. Still, he taught, preached, and healed, and in the process deepened the faith of those around him. His enemies eventually gained power, and after pursuing him throughout his ministry, gained enough power to have him killed, hoping that this would put an end to his ideas. Yet this didn't stop him. He overcame his own death and created an even greater movement that became Christianity, and continues to grow and thrive today. Successful pastoral leaders often follow similar plotlines in their ministry. They come to a congregation, and many love them. But there are doubters and possibly Judases in their midst. They face a crisis that could bring down their ministry. But somehow, despite going through a period that feels like it will lead to death, they find a way to bring about new life. And by the gift of the Spirit, the community grows. They craft a story with their leadership.

Structure

Good narrative always has a particular structure. According to McKee, the structure isn't just the technical structure of the drama (that is, the scenes that make up the acts, and the acts that make up the plot). Each scene has an internal structure. Some meaningful transformation in the character always takes place in each scene. The character faces some challenge, and she is transformed in response to it. For instance, she may undergo a change from healthy to unhealthy, from confident to confused, from fallen and broken to redeemed, or from uncertain to convicted. Typically, the change in the scene is minor and perhaps only barely noticeable, but a shift occurs that the character recognizes, even if this transformational shift isn't readily apparent. In each act, the series of changes cumulate to create a major transformation or a shift of values, either from something positive to something negative or vice versa. The Bible follows this structure fairly consistently. For instance, each story has particular scenes that chronicle the shifts in the characters from unfaithful to faithful, fearful to faithful, prideful to humble, humble to glorified, lost to found, unsaved to saved, blind to seeing, and much more.

In my own experience, I have found that each week in the life of a congregation, each worship service, pretty much every meeting in the church, and each personal interaction between pastor and member has the potential for a "scenelike" transition that over time culminates in major "act" shifts. What I mean by this is that each event of the congregation has in it the opportunity to lead the congregation into a transformation, either positive or negative.

Adrian van Kaam, a writer in the area of spiritual formation, talks about these small transformations, especially those that are positive. He calls them "just noticeable improvements."[9] Just noticeable improvements are the tiny life shifts that each of us notices as we grow in positive directions. Congregations that grow in a healthy direction are always experiencing these just noticeable improvements as they emerge out of worship, meetings, education, small groups, and casual interactions. They become the scenes of a church, while each liturgical season or each year become much like acts in a play. The pastor, acting as leader, becomes the facilitator of these shifts by leading in a narrative way, helping the congregation script new scenes, new acts, and new plays. And the pastor also points out these shifts to the congregation, making the just noticeable shifts much more noticeable. They talk of these shifts in personal conversations, newsletter articles, committee and board meetings, and in sermons and classes.

The best pastoral leaders seem to be able to take struggles inherent within congregations—discussions over budgeting, program, a problem member of the church, a leak in the roof—and transform them into opportunities. The best leaders always lead others toward transformational shifts in which even the most insignificant interactions can create the context for slight transformations of people and the congregation. These leaders don't facilitate the shifts through micromanaging. Instead, they create the context through leadership in which transformational expectations are created, and people expect to be transformed by worship, education, meetings, and other events of the church. Poor leaders face the struggles of a church and seem to move from placidity to conflict. It is as though they only know how to follow a dysfunctional shift, leading a congregation from dysfunction to deeper dysfunction.

These leaders seem to inherently know whether a situation fits with the plot they are scripting and how to let things go that don't fit the plot, how to trust that the process will find its way back into the plot or how to move the situation back into harmony with the plot. Part of their inherent knowing has to do with their ability to recognize certain essentials. For instance, they understand that endings, even if it is the ending of a meeting or a service or a moment, must lead to resolution immersed in reconciliation and redemption. They understand that conflict must be resolved with forgiveness. And they understand that agreement must be sought in a way that respects differences.

Ultimately, narrative pastoral leaders understand their own stories and their congregations' stories, and they are good at doing something that Malcolm Gladwell calls "thin-slicing" in each situation, as they assess whether they are still on-script or off-script. Thin-slicing is a basically unconscious act that all of us engage in all the time. It is a tiny moment of time when our unconscious discovers patterns in situations and behaviors based on a very narrow slice of experience, but it discovers it in a way that leads to a full recognition of the truth of a situation.[10] Thin-slicing, for instance, is what a policeman does when he drives by an innocent-looking situation but still senses that something is wrong. It allows an art appraiser to know at a glance that a painting is a forgery, even though the painting is perfect in every way. It enables a comedian to immediately know what is funny in an improvisational situation. It also enables a pastoral leader to inherently know when a situation is on-script or off-script. And the more adept at leadership a pastor becomes, through training and experience, the more she is able to recognize what the situation entails and how to move it back on-script. In doing so, she is able to sort through all sorts of extraneous information that stymies or confuses most others. Her ability to thin-slice and assess a situation isn't just natural and unconscious. The best leaders are also training junkies. They understand that they need to constantly refine their perspectives through reading, training, and education. And the more they refine them, the more they see with clarity at unconscious levels, levels where their perspective integrates intellect, emotion, intuition, training, and knowledge.

Transformation

In my own leadership, I have noticed, I am always looking for *transformation*. I want each worship service, for instance, to create the opportunity for the positive transformation of people so that they can grow closer to what God is calling them to be. I look at each meeting as a chance to go from where we are to where God is leading us to go. I see many personal interactions, whether with members or with staff, as an opportunity to move them through transformation. And I see the events of my own life unfolding in that way that transforms me. I have noticed that effective leaders always seem to embrace their own transformation, even if it is painful.

I have been highlighting this already, but I want to make this even more explicit. Transformation is always taking place in a congregation, and it can either be positive or negative. In all good narratives, transformation takes place throughout the course of the story. With all good leadership, positive transformation takes place throughout the life of the congregation. With ineffective leadership, negative transformation takes place. The key is that an ineffective leader often feels trapped in dysfunction, not able to see the possibility for positive transformation. He might blame himself. He might blame the congregation. He might blame the denomination. Or he might blame the culture.

Whatever he blames, he sees no possibility, and thus suffers from a leadership writer's block.

Effective congregational leaders are always leading the congregation and its members into positive transformation. It can be spiritual transformation, missional transformation, physical transformation, or communal transformation. Often it is a mixture of them all. The key to the transformation is often that both the leaders and the congregations get there due to some mild or extensive crisis—exterior or interior, communal or personal. Most congregations and their leaders try to avoid pain and crises, yet when they do, they also miss opportunities. These pains and crises can actually be the contexts in which positive transformations take place. Healthy narrative leaders don't necessarily hide from crises, but see crises as opportunities to script healthy outcomes. There is nothing more powerful and nurturing to the life of a congregation than a story of it entering a crisis, and then finding a way to something better because it persevered, overcame all obstacles, and discovered a much better way of living and being. Healthy narrative pastors lead congregations through crises to something better. They don't want to go through periods of crisis, but they also recognize the inherent positive potential of crises.

Look at Harry Truman's leadership at the end of World War II. At the end of wars in the past, the typical reaction of the victorious country was to punish and subjugate the defeated country, much like what was done to Germany at the end of World War I. Truman led the United States and the Allies to react differently: to bring about reconciliation and redemption through aid to Germany and Japan. By doing so, he transformed those countries as well as the United States. It transformed America by giving the country a narrative that this is now a nation that forgives. He was building on a previous narrative in which Abraham Lincoln led the Union to forgive the Confederate States. All the great U.S. presidents led the country to positive transformation. Some through war, others through domestic crises. The worst leaders led the United States through negative transformation. The mediocre leaders? They led the country through no transformation. To be a great leader means to lead people through positive transformation.

Pastor as Narrative Leader

To be a narrative leader means to be something very similar to a novel writer. It means to be able to see not only life in general, but also a congregation's life, as an unfolding story that to some extent she is the author of. Obviously the pastor is not the author, but then again, most writers of fiction will tell you that they are not truly the authors of their stories either. Listen to how an author describes the writing experience. Often she will say that she gets a general idea of the plot and the characters, but over time the story begins to tell itself. She will say that the characters determine the direction. She will say that it feels as though someone else is writing the story through her. The same is true for pastoral leaders.

Many writers also speak of writing as a process of listening to their muse. In Greek mythology, the muses were nine daughters of Zeus who inspired artists, poets, sculptors, and the likes. Present-day artists speak of their muses as being almost like spiritual voices that inspire them. Pastors also have a muse: Christ. The more open we pastors are to the Spirit as we lead, the more the Spirit guides us not only to craft our own story, or the congregation's story, but also to make these stories part of the larger story that God is writing about life throughout the universe. The great pastoral leaders write a story discerned through prayer.

As the author listening to his muse, the pastor recognizes when the congregation is or isn't meshing with God's story. And he finds a way to bring it back into harmony. At the same time, he still sees pain, crisis, death, birth, divorce, marriage, difficulty, and celebration as crucial elements of the story. He understands that without these elements, the story has no life. As a result, he is always looking for ways to turn the more difficult situations into times of redemption, reconciliation, and resurrection.

While the pastor acts as the author, he also understands that he is something of the main character and narrator of the story. I don't mean this in some narcissistic way in which the pastor *must* be the main focus or that everything revolves around him. In fact, that is generally not the case in the best narrative leaders. The best leaders are able to *let* a congregation's story unfold, as I said before. The leader is not the center, but he is the person who bears the most responsibility for attending to the story and ensuring that it follows the narrative. The pastor acts as narrator, sometimes merely observing, monitoring, and articulating what others are doing and sometimes acting as a character involved in the action. The key thing is that as narrator, the pastor is responsible for framing and articulating the events. The pastor provides an interpretation. And that interpretation comes through many avenues. It may be an interpretation of an event told in a sermon. It may be an interpretation of an event given by the pastor to leaders in committee and board meetings. Or it may simply be an interpretation the pastor gives as he talks casually with members. Whatever the means, the pastor recounts an event, and then teaches others through story how to understand it. Let me give you an example.

Recently, the school district in the Zelienople area had a contract dispute that led the teachers to go on strike. I had been told several years ago that a previous strike in the 1980s came close to dividing the church. The congregation has always had a fair number of teachers in it, and in 1985 tempers boiled over in the church. Many parents and teachers became embroiled in conflict with each other. And some of the parents did things that clearly were not Christian in their behavior.

Not only wanting to prevent a potential crisis with this present strike but also seeing an opportunity to script an alternative story—a story of Christian love in the midst of division—I sent an e-mail to members and placed a letter in the church bulletin, calling on all members to remember that they are Christians first, and that it is in times like these that we are called upon to act even more Christian, for Christian behavior is nurtured most in crisis. I invited them to read the words of Ephesians 4:1–6, in which Paul reminds all of us to "lead a life worthy of the calling to which you have been called, with all humility and gentleness, with patience, bearing with one another in love, making every effort to maintain the unity of the Spirit," as well as Philippians 2:1–5, in which Paul reminds us to "be of the same mind, having the same love, being in full accord and of one mind. Do nothing from selfish ambition or conceit, but in humility regard others as better than yourselves." The whole point was that we were to be people of love first, whatever our opinion was.

After the second worship service, a man who used to be a member of the congregation, having moved away fifteen years earlier, and who was visiting that Sunday, came up to me and said, "I need to talk with you about your insert in the bulletin. Twenty years ago when we had the last strike, I acted in a way that wasn't Christian. My faith was really immature then. I wish we had had something like this in the bulletin then because I did things that really killed some very important relationships that I had. I don't think the folks from back then have ever forgiven me, and it bothers me. I really appreciate your writing this." What is interesting is that he told other members of the church the same thing.

Some of them came up to me to tell me what he had said to them, and I told them that he had said the same thing to me. Then we all remarked on how interesting and coincidental and providential it was that he happened to show up on that very Sunday. Why did he pick that Sunday to visit and not any other over the previous ten years? We agreed that God was doing something, that God was transforming him and us. The providence of this situation is that this small story is now part of our church's narrative, which is a narrative of God's Spirit, redemption, and reconciliation. But it is also an affirmation of what I was trying to do, which is to teach love in the midst of division. Because the man told so many people, I can now use that story to tell others how God works in ways to bring about reconciliation and transformation. I become a narrator, using the story to move the church along a redemptive plotline.

A final thought on how the pastor acts as narrative leader: the good pastoral leader also seems to find a way to separate himself from the story in order to steer the story in a particular direction. While he may be the narrator, he also is something of the author, and like an author he is able to keep himself from becoming so trapped in the story's events that he becomes a helpless victim of the story. He does not let himself become trapped in a careening plot that ambles towards dysfunction and meaninglessness. Instead, he is able to see the story both from within and without. He is able to be both a subjective participant in the story and an objective observer of events who leads the story back into God's story.

Ultimately, being a pastoral, narrative leader means to be a leader who is both immersed in the events of a church and, at the same time, an author of the congregation, leading the church to follow the plot that she or he believes God has scripted for the congregation. It means understanding the Christian story well enough to be able to move the congregation to follow the Christian narrative, which is a narrative of life, growth, turmoil, death, resurrection, redemption, and reconciliation.

Notes

1. Daniel H. Pink, *A Whole New Mind: Why Right-Brainers Will Rule the Future* (New York: Riverhead Books, 2005), 102.

2. Ibid., 14.

3. Donald A. Norman, *Things that Make Us Smart: Defending Human Attributes in the Age of the Machine* (New York: Perseus Books, 1993), 146.

4. Joseph Campbell and Bill Moyers, *The Power of Myth* (New York: Doubleday, 1988), 5–6.

5. Based on Lev Grossman, "How Apple Does It," Time.com, October 16, 2005, http://www.time.com/time/magazine/article/0,9171,1118384-1,00.html, and "Apple, Inc.," Wikipedia, http://en.wikipedia.org/wiki/Apple_Inc.

6. Robert McKee, *Story: Substance, Structure, Style, and the Principles of Screenwriting* (New York: Regan Books, 1997).

7. Ibid., 4–5.

8. Ibid., 48–49.

9. Adrian van Kaam and Susan Muto, *The Power of Appreciation: A New Approach to Personal and Relational Healing* (New York: Crossroad, 1993), 28.

10. Malcolm Gladwell, *Blink: The Power of Thinking without Thinking* (New York: Little Brown, 2005), 23.

CHAPTER 4

The Sacred Value
of Congregational Stories

~

TIM SHAPIRO

People everywhere tell stories, but people in congregations tell many stories. The congregation I served for more than fourteen years told many stories about Geneva Williams. Almost every one of the three hundred members had a Geneva Williams story. Janet told the story of how Geneva started an intercessory prayer group that met every week in Geneva's home. Harold described how the antiques in Geneva's house were worth as much as the house itself.

Lori from the youth group described what Geneva did when she was no longer able to attend worship. For many years Lori sat behind Geneva in worship. During the passing of the peace, Lori would say, "I love your red hat." Geneva always, always wore the same red hat to worship. The week Lori was confirmed in the church she received a package from Geneva, now homebound. In the package was Geneva's red hat.

Everyone had a Geneva story. When Geneva died, there wasn't only one eulogy; there were a dozen because so many people testified to the mark she made on their life. Once the youth group went Christmas caroling. They had seven stops to make. Halfway through the evening, they rang Geneva's doorbell. She opened the door and stood there with a beautiful smile. The youth sang "Joy to the World." Geneva said, "You must come in." "Oh, no," the youth leader said. "We don't want to interrupt your evening." "I insist," said Geneva. She had, by now, stepped out on the porch. With cane in hand, she was herding the youth into the living room.

"Let me get you something to eat."

One of the youth said, "We can't stay long."

"Oh, you will be on your way soon enough," hollered Geneva from the kitchen.

Over the next ten minutes she brought out cake, ice cream, oranges, Oreos, Hostess Twinkies, milk, saltwater taffy, leftover noodles from her supper, dinner rolls, olives, and marshmallows. She lit a candle and began to tell stories. She described Christmas Eve at the old downtown sanctuary: the poinsettias, she said, matched the color of her hat. She read from Psalm 46, her favorite. When the conversation started to fade, she offered more food ("I can't eat these Oreos by myself") and began a new story.

All kinds of stories are told in congregations. This is the way it goes, day in and day out with people who participate in congregational life. After all, this is what humans do. They tell stories. People in congregations are, in this way, no different from people in other settings.

The Use of Stories in Congregations

Stories dwell in congregational life amid a theology of revelation. Stories told in congregations reveal how God is at work among the people. Stories report the practices most valued by a particular congregation. The telling of stories in congregational life has extrinsic value as they facilitate new insight and action. But more than that, simply telling them has intrinsic value. The use and function of narrative in congregations is important not because it leads to something else but simply for its own sake. Such narratives, even when the subject has to do with difficult things like loss and conflict, witness to God's presence in the unfolding of human life. Congregational narratives reveal God at work. God's work is revealed in the practices embedded in stories that reflect a particular life together. The stories, and the practices described in the stories, are homeland for God's Spirit. Craig Dykstra, senior vice president for religion at Lilly Endowment, observes that "The practices of Christian faith turn out in the end not primarily to be practices, efforts. They turn out to be places in the contours of our personal and communal lives where a habitation of the Spirit is able to occur."[1]

Consider a congregation, any congregation. On the day of worship, the preacher weaves stories through her sermon. Some of the stories are about people the listeners don't know; some are about people who live in their neighborhood. After worship, as coffee is poured and children reach for donut holes, more stories are told. Storytelling takes place one-on-one and in accidental small groups. What happened at work this week? How is it going after surgery? Where has the Smith family been the last month?

Sunday is over and the rest of the week brings more stories. These stories are heard during pastoral calls, in small group meetings, and while people linger in the church office. Some of these stories are private, so they are told in confidence. Many of the stories could be categorized as personal testimony because they describe events that are meaningful and poignant, and they carry an intuitive revelation of truth. God is present between the lines of the story even if God isn't a primary, named character. The stories relate the congregation's life beyond the official structure of organizational life. Each story, private or public, adds material to the composition of congregational life.

In addition to personal witness, people tell stories about institutional experiences of faith. Personal witness often relays experiences of everyday life that do not need the sanction of congregational life; but stories of institutional experiences of faith describe human life connected with the congregation's practices and official programs. People share these stories during committee or board meetings, in the pastor's office, or at annual meetings. Such congregational stories are often less overtly about faith and more about the organizational health or traditions of the congregation. Clergy new to a congregation hear these stories as do visitors. The stories may be about what happened when the previous pastor divorced and moved or when the fire destroyed the education wing. Some of these stories affirm the current state of the congregation, while others challenge the status quo.

The congregation I served even had a Geneva story that reflected institutional change. The church had been through a difficult time. People were angry with each other. More than a few members had left the church. Several resigned from the governing board. Members of the nominating committee were looking for people to fill remaining terms. Someone said, "Let's nominate Geneva to fill Donald's place." At this point Geneva was almost eighty years old. "Is she too old?" one person asked. "Not for this term," the chair of the committee said. "Donald's term expires in three months." So Geneva was nominated, elected, and served three months as an elder. At the end of her term another elder reported, "She served with distinction."

The Narrative Quality of Life

Scholar Stephen Crites's contribution to the book *Why Narrative?* examined the narrative quality of life itself.[2] When people tell stories, they do more than create a plot; they represent an innate quality of existence. Life is essentially narrative-like. Stories include movement through time, characters, and dramatic tension, among other attributes. So does the experience of life. What happened next? Who did what? How did that get resolved? The answers to those questions are key elements of a story and they are key elements of everyday life.

Crites describes three aspects of the narrative quality of existence. He identifies three narrative tracks: "sacred stories, mundane stories and the temporal form of experience itself."[3]

Sacred stories shape human activity, often in unconscious ways. Sacred stories are formative and stand on their own. That is, they exist above or beyond time, resistant to the forces of culture. They are powerful even if we are not aware of their power. Sacred stories are so woven into community life that they have power without being articulated. When told, they often take the form of ritual representation such as the story of the Last Supper, which is retold as part of a communion liturgy. Sacred stories aren't so much rewritten as they are almost beyond editing. What is more likely is that a community will change so that it inhabits a different narrative, a different sacred story.

Mundane stories are powerful too, Crites reminds us. The word *mundane*, like *sacred*, is more descriptive than literal. I prefer the word *ordinary*, or *common*. People are much more conscious of mundane stories than sacred ones. Mundane stories are rooted overtly in particular times and places. The stories told in a Ken Burns documentary fit Crites's description of mundane exactly because they describe and explain why and how certain experiences develop. They are not boring, as *mundane* sometimes means. They are engaging because people identify with them and see how they inform a person's life experience. People tell mundane stories about all kinds of things. These are the stories people tell about their lives: going to the store, going to work, what happened today.

According to Crites, the narrative expression of life includes not only sacred and mundane stories but also the *experience* of life itself. The ebb and flow of each day represents the narrative quality of existence. Life involves memory, which includes consciousness of the passage of time and the way life unfolds from one moment to the next. Life involves engagement with people: those we meet each day, those we meet only once, those from our past, and even projections of people we have yet to meet.

Certainly, congregations are subject to this story-shaped world. Crites's description of the narrative quality of existence and the three different forms of narrative is helpful in understanding congregational life. His analysis applies to all of life, including congregations.

Congregations live by one or more sacred stories. The sacred story will, with varying degrees of awareness in the congregation, influence congregational life. Typically, a congregation will reflect in its practices a particular sacred story or at least a dominant theme from a sacred story. A congregation particularly gifted in hospitality may be living out Genesis 18, Abraham and Sarah welcoming three visitors who foretell the birth of Isaac. In addition, complementary and contradictory sacred stories can influence practice. They affect the ongoing, negotiated contours of community life. Sacred stories include Bible narratives that are particularly authoritative, even if the clergy and laity are not aware the texts carry such authority. Even though such texts are not read every week in worship, often an indirect or ritual expression of the story is present in the congregation's life. What makes a story sacred for a congregation is its subterranean power to influence the practice of the faith community. Such stories rest beneath what is openly revealed or avowed. Their sacredness comes from the reality that they are hidden *and* powerful.

It is possible that the sacred story of the congregation comes from a text other than Scripture. In the United States, many congregations carry certain stories from the American narrative in their institutional bloodstream. One Midwest congregation I know has a large Fourth of July pageant. Each year a new drama is written by one of the congregation's members. Actors are recruited. Music is written and rehearsed. The event sells out. Attendance for the pageant is greater than for the congregation's Easter or Christmas services. Affirming the American story through these Independence Day dramas is authoritative for this community's life. As with most sacred stories, the expression of the story in congregational life is indirect. It is representational as opposed to literal. The congregation doesn't read from the Constitution during worship; instead they represent some aspect of this sacred story through drama. The Fourth of July festival is not itself a sacred story, but it represents the unpronounced sacred narrative that influences the congregation's life together.

Applying Crites's categories, congregations also live by mundane stories. These mundane stories are not boring, if told well, but are common or ordinary in the sense that they relate to everyday life and do not require special knowledge or special privilege for participation in the telling and listening. Some mundane stories are public and some are private. These stories can be abundant and long lasting in a congregation's life, in part because they are open to interpretation. They may change in form or meaning through the years. They form consciousness and are formed by consciousness.

In her novel *Saint Maybe*, writer Anne Tyler tells the story of Ian Bedloe, a young man who through a series of tragic events becomes the guardian of his brother's and sister-in-law's children.[4] He finds support, encouragement, and fleeting solace from the people and pastor of Church of the Second Chance, a storefront church that is the spiritual home for people whose lives are far from settled. Life at Church of the Second Chance is richly depicted in the novel, and many congregations can see their story in the book.

The first time Ian attends the church he hears a strange story told during prayer requests. A grieving mother tells how her son died while serving in the military. He jumped from a plane without a parachute. The mother says to the other worshipers, "This soldier tells me it's the army's considered opinion that Chuckie had just jumped so often, he'd stopped thinking about it."[5] Ian is not sure what to make of such an unusual place, where strange stories are told and where people listen to them as if their strangeness were universal. He discovers that such stories are common in this congregation, and in time he finds himself telling faith stories too.

Mundane stories represent sacred things but are not sacred in themselves. They are powerful but they are not all-powerful. That is, the teller has some control over how the stories affect a community. The stories about Geneva Williams in her red hat and the stories about life at Church of the Second Chance are mundane stories, in Crites's terms, because they represent the everyday life of congregations. They are mundane stories because they are mutable. Mundane stories are open to interpretation and change as life itself changes over time. Mundane stories are abundant in congregational life and so they appear ordinary. Yet they contain a richness and complexity that reflects the richness and complexity of ordinary life.

Congregational life possesses a narrative quality, which is prominently reflected in the passage of time. One Lord's Day moves towards the next. Liturgical seasons approach and then pass. The first church I preached in had a large grandfather clock in the sanctuary. As I put on my robe, I pointed to the clock just as it rang for the quarter hour and asked my host, "Is that so I don't run too long?" He said, "Oh, no, you can run as long as you like. It's for us. It lets us know when our roasts are done back home and whether or not we need to get up and out of here. But you, you can go as long as you like."

Time marches on, and so does life. Congregational stories hold a kind of luminous, performative space between fiction and nonfiction—between the telling of a story and the unfolding of an event. Two of Crites's categories of narrative—mundane stories and experience as story—often merge so that it is hard to tell the difference from one to another. When is the telling of an experience distinct from experience itself? This in-between space can be particularly rich with meaning in congregational settings where the telling of a story is linked with the continuation of the congregation's narrative and the ongoing revelation of God.

A plot development in Anne Tyler's *Saint Maybe* reveals the synchronicity between real life and common stories. Sometime after the deaths of his brother and sister-in-law, Ian Bedloe talks with Reverend Emmett about forgiveness. Ian is trying to determine to what extent he should be responsible for the couple's children. Also, can he be forgiven for his role, however minor, in his brother's death? Reverend Emmett suggests that Ian needs to pay reparation. Ian needs to see after the children. After all, as Reverend Emmett says, "God wants to know how far you'll go to undo the harm you've done."[6]

Indeed, for the next several years, Ian sacrifices most all of his dreams to care for the children. Years later, when Ian is wrestling with another major decision, he has a different conversation with Reverend Emmett. Uncharacteristically, Ian complains:

"*This* is my life? This is all I get? It's so settled! It's so cut and dried! After this there's no changing! I just lean into the burden of these children forever, is that what you're saying?"

"No," Reverend Emmett told him.

"You said that! You said to lean into my burden!"

"But those children will be grown in no time," Reverend Emmett said. "*They* are not the burden I meant. The burden is forgiveness."

"Okay," Ian said, "Fine. How much longer till I'm forgiven?"

"No, no. The burden is that *you* must forgive."

"Me?" Ian said. He stared at Reverend Emmett. "Forgive who?"

"Why, your brother and his wife, of course."[7]

This story takes place in a congregational context. Imagine how it might be shared, not in a novel but as part of congregational gossip or testimony: "Poor, Ian, he takes care of those children." These episodes demonstrate how life and narrative unfold over time so that both take on new meaning as time moves along.

At first, and for many years, Ian believes he needs to be forgiven. Later, he finds out that he is the one who must forgive. To the reader it appears as if Reverend Emmett is giving him opposing advice. Did Reverend Emmett misspeak years earlier? Or did Ian hear him wrong? The story is ambiguous just as real life is.

The common stories of a congregation and the actual experiences of the congregation sometimes match and they sometimes clash. Even when they clash, they function like individual human experience; they shape memory and reveal digressions, regrets, and minds that are changing much of the time.

Ambiguous Revelation

Storytelling is intrinsically important to congregations because stories mirror the ambiguity of life while also providing revelation of God's presence. Their intrinsic value is in the sense of connection, the grasp of life's richness, the desire for God represented by the narrative as well as the act of storytelling.

Just as a relationship exists between congregational narratives and the lived experience of the congregation, a connection also exists between congregational narratives and Scripture. Congregational narratives continue and extend Scripture. The first words of the Gospel of Mark read, "The beginning of the good news of Jesus Christ, the Son of God" (1:1). What does "the beginning" mean? The beginning could be the start of the book itself; or it could be the appearance of John the Baptist whose proclamation soon follows (vv. 4–8); or it could be the baptism of Jesus, which is also described very near the start of the book (vv. 9–11).

But here is another possibility. The beginning to which Mark refers might be the entire gospel movement, the lived experience of faith in people's lives. In a sense, the story of faith is always beginning. To put it another way, the good news of faith is like a story that is "to be continued." The life of faith does not find a neat and tidy end at the conclusion of the Gospel. The story carries on.

The conclusion of Mark's Gospel is open-ended. The original version concludes with the enigmatic words, "And they said nothing to anyone, for they were afraid" (16:8).[8] What do these words mean? Did the women tell anyone that Christ was risen? And if they did not, as the witness suggests, how did others hear the news? Wouldn't those who heard the Markan witness wonder how they themselves came to hear if, because of fear, no one spoke? What kind of nonconclusive ending is this?

Perhaps Mark's introduction and abbreviated ending intend to blaze a mutable path, not a closed trail. Mark tells his Gospel with an abbreviated ending so that the listeners might sense that they are part of the "to be continued" project called faith. Mark ends the narrative in midsentence because there is no ending. The ending, or more accurately the continuation of the narrative, is in the life of the faith communities that follow. The Gospel of Mark is a book without an ending. The narrative continues in the stories told by contemporary congregations.

Robert Kegan reflects on this view of the unending quality to stories. He writes:

> The Jewish mystics say that God makes human beings because God loves stories. This is quite a modest stance to give an all-powerful, all-loving God. Even God, the mystics are saying, does not know how we are going to come out, so why should we wish for greater control or need it? Better perhaps for us to emulate this kind of god, whose pleasure in us comes

not from our obedience to God's laws and regularities, however subject we may be to them, but from God's sheer fascina-
tion with how we will live.

For a God like this one, we ourselves are the objects of
passionate engagement, endlessly let go of and recovered for
a purpose God himself (or God herself) may not yet know.
We ourselves are endlessly let go of and recovered as we, all
the while, reverberate against the garage door and throughout
the House.[9]

Stories as Narrated Practices

Stories reflect the narrative quality of congregational life. Stories told by congregants and their leaders reflect the continuing
story of Scripture. Such stories also provide evidence of the
ways of faith most valued by a particular congregation. The
stories told by congregants reveal the lived theology of a faith
community. *Congregational stories are narrated practices.*

Storytelling is important to congregations not as another
strategy for vitality or tool for assessment but because it reveals meaning and practices. In this sense, stories are a primary
form God's revelation assumes in congregational life. Stories
provide richer data than demographic information. Stories
provide deeper insights than congregational surveys. They are
more than a technique or a tool to interpret a congregation.
Stories reveal the structures of everyday existence. They are not
a perfect replica of real life, but then nothing is. Because they
reveal the structure of everyday existence, they are the primary
way to understand the meaning of congregational life. Because
people relive experience through stories, they are a fundamen-
tal way to sustain congregational life. When stories are shared,
the encounter with experience they provide has the effect of
defining and sustaining that particular way of life. Ultimately,

God's revelation exists in the structure of a congregation's way of life. The structure becomes apparent in the telling and hearing of stories.

Embedded in congregational narratives are traces and markers of faith practices. Practice is how people do things. The practices of faith are how people of faith do things. Thinking about faith practices involves thinking about activities common to humanity. Practices common to humanity are considered as faith practices when applied by faithful people who are conscious of their faith story, a story that is personal and corporate. Practices don't include just any activity, though many activities can make up a particular practice. Faith practices are unique and varied expressions of essential, deep-rooted activities done by people who thoughtfully, actively, and competently embody their faith with and for others. Such practices include hospitality, shaping community, healing, singing, dying well, saying yes and saying no, and discernment.[10]

Telling congregational stories is a particular form of faith practice called testimony. All kinds of stories exist in and beyond congregations. People tell stories not only in sanctuaries but also at the dinner table, on the playground, and at presidential debates. Testimony is the broader description of stories people tell that relate the truth of human experience. Testimony is a practice that happens all the time in many different settings. Testimony is a *faith* practice when it occurs within a faith community or when the content of the testimony has to do with faith. Like other activities connected to faith practice, a tradition or history informs the storytelling. Standards of excellence exist; some people are better storytellers than others. Within a congregation, the history, the health, and the context of the congregation form and reform the kinds of stories told.

The way stories are told and heard certainly shapes the practices of a congregation. Stories and practices are mutually informing. A complex spiritual, psychological, and educational dynamic occurs when stories are told. The clearest way to

describe this dynamic is to highlight the performative and ex-
periential aspect of narrative. People learn by experience, by
doing. Stories are the next best thing to being there.

The congregation I served hosted a particularly active intercessory prayer group. It was actually a renegade group as it never carried board approval as an official program. Clearly, prayer
was an important discipline to these people. They weren't going
to let the lack of official sanction stop them. For this group,
intercessory prayer was essential to the practice of healing.

While only a few from the congregation participated in the
group, participants told stories to others in the congregation
about what the prayer group did. Through the stories, many
more experienced the practice of prayer. People told how Geneva Williams served as their host. Picture her greeting people
at the door of her home (without the red hat—this wasn't Sunday morning). They told how she served refreshments between
the Bible readings and the concentrated prayer time. Participants argued, sometimes heatedly, about Scripture ("Don't tell
me this is the ending of Mark!"). In their prayers they shared
concerns about particular people. People told stories about
what dessert Geneva made them eat until the serving plate
was empty. Stories about the experience reinforced the importance of the experience, evidence that stories and practices exist
together in a kind of holy symmetry.

The practice of prayer—and the stories told about it—
highlighted the interest the congregation had in this form of
ministry. The stories prayer group members told about their
prayer practice reinforced the interest of participants and
others in the church. The narratives served as the syntax of a
deepening practice.

Stories, whether oral or written, reveal practice. The structure of everyday life that stories reveal is the structure of
practice. This idea is parallel to Marianne Sawicki's proposal
that Scripture functions as inscribed practice.[11] Biblical texts
describe events but they also describe predominant practices

of the community from which they came. In her book *Seeing the Lord*, Sawicki suggests that resurrection passages describe what the first Christians were doing when they most deeply sensed the presence of the risen Christ. Resurrection texts include meals—the breakfast at Galilee, the dinner at Emmaus— because early Christians experienced the risen Christ while feeding the hungry. The talent for knowing a hungry person when you see one is a prerequisite for seeing the risen Lord. The practice of feeding the hungry leads one to encounter Jesus Christ. So, resurrection stories have authority as they become inscribed not only in a sacred book but also on bodies, on the lives of people seeking to live faithfully.

Stories of Jesus's resurrection do not point to some golden day never to be repeated. They are stories to be inscribed on the heart, as when Jeremiah wrote that the covenant should be written on their hearts (Jer. 31:33). Sawicki's interpretation of resurrection texts state that such faith practices as feeding the hungry are not outcomes of faith but preconditions for it.[12]

Much of the time congregants think of Bible narratives as pointing to particular practices that they should emulate. The assumption is that texts come first. People's responses to the texts, among other variables, lead then to particular practices. But what if practices come first? What if Scripture texts exist in the canon not only because of the event's power but also because the practice revealed or hidden in the text was crucial to the faith community's identity and function? Practices are inscribed from lived experience. The original texts were people's lives and were not Scripture. Bible texts were lived practices before they were words on the page. Doing is the first act. The practices of faith are the supporting structure, even the supporting revelation, of the sacred story of Scripture.

No wonder Scripture contains so many different forms of storytelling—history, gospel, apocalypse, and so on. Scripture captures the wide variety of human experience with God as it developed many centuries ago. Stories told in congregations reveal the practices most honored by the congregation. They reveal the tradition of the practice, standards of excellence for the practice, the varied conditions and virtues that produce the practice, and the goods the practice produces.

I visited a small rural congregation with stories to tell about children. I walked into the sanctuary escorted by a lanky farmer. He pointed to the many pictures on the wall. "This painting was donated by the Langdon family," he said. It was a painting of Jesus with the disciples at the Last Supper. "They lost their child Danny to leukemia." He explained that the five other paintings in the sanctuary were also memorial gifts, each from a family in memory of a young child who had died.

My host told a story about each child, about the illness or accident that took the young person's life and how the family had managed or understandably stumbled through the years. The stories were like personal passion narratives. The stories sounded rehearsed, but not perfunctory. They had been told before. Each of the stories described the way the church members participated with and for the families in practices of healing and of dying well.

Telling these stories in my presence revealed and affirmed their congregational practice. The stories demonstrated the virtues of care and remembrance that shaped their practice. Each of the stories included ways in which the church shared the family's burden. For one family, the harvest was completed by church members without them having to ask. My host elaborated, "Picture five combines in the field until past midnight." For another family, meals were brought every night during a long hospital stay. "We're not doctors but we know how to make fried chicken."

One of the grieving fathers began drinking too much. Something very close to a therapeutic intervention was designed, but all the participants were members of the church. The intervention was received with good grace but proved unsuccessful. My farmer host described the aftermath with disappointment but without judgment, which intrigued me. "Ben is one of my best friends. I don't know how he makes it through the day."

These stories are told to most everyone who asks about the pictures on the sanctuary walls. They are not secrets. This particular congregation has been in existence since 1841, and the sanctuary has been standing almost that long. They must have a hundred different stories to tell a visitor. But it is these stories of grief and attempted healing that are told. They reveal that practices of healing surrounding the rites of death are particularly meaningful and abundant in this community. For this community, moving toward grief, rather than denying it, is important, as are sharing burdens and withholding judgment. These practices are revealed in the congregation's stories.

The Goods of Storytelling

What does this mean for congregations? They must know that practices produce extrinsic and intrinsic goods. Stories, as part of the larger practice of testimony, relate in narrative form the practices honored by a congregation. Likewise, storytelling and listening that reveals the lived practice of a congregation produces external and internal goods just as other practices do.[13]

The extrinsic goods of storytelling in a congregation are manifested in an achieved end or goal. The end or goal may be related to maintaining a vital congregation. The stories told in a congregation may help the community live out its mission. The circulation of stories may provide an environ that helps people be faithful to their understanding of Scripture. Storytelling in congregations creates a sense of shared identity. Storytelling and listening can help a congregation think and act strategically.

For example, some clergy use a particular type of preaching called roundtable preaching.[14] The sermon roundtable refers to a small group of people gathered to brainstorm ideas about a sermon that will be preached by the pastor. A group of eight to twelve people meets early in the week to discuss the upcoming sermon. Together they interpret the Scripture text. They talk about how the text relates to their life. By doing so, they tell stories about their lives. The preacher, with permission, can weave the stories told at the roundtable gathering into the sermon. The assembled congregation overhears testimony from others.

Many extrinsic goods result from such stories. Such testimony is met with curiosity and full attention. Parishioners listen closely to the experiences of others with whom they share congregational life. Everyday stories serve as examples of how the meaning of particular Scripture texts gets mapped onto people's lives. Also, these local stories move the sermon from argument or apologetic to affirming God's presence in life as it is here and now.

The most powerful use of stories in congregations is ingeniously nonutilitarian. The extrinsic goods are important, but they are not where the whole action is. Stories have the rare power to shape human life simply in being told, regardless of what strategies or manipulations are employed. Indeed, framing congregational stories as a continuation of Scripture and as narration of reality and revelation makes the intrinsic goods just as meaningful, and maybe more so, as the extrinsic ones. After all, practices are most powerful when the practitioner participates in them for their own sake. Storytelling in congregations is most powerful when it is appreciated for its intrinsic value. Here is some advice: In short, don't mess with a congregation's stories; don't stage-manage them; let them breathe on their own.

Congregational stories are sacred, not in the Stephen Crites sense, but in the sense that they are powerful, and only with great restraint should they be manipulated or tinkered with. They are like the Ark of the Covenant. When someone tells a story, listeners should pay heed in a way that Uzzah the Levite never did (2 Sam. 6:1–7).[15] Don't touch. Don't tinker. Instead, listen and learn. The stories that people tell about their life and the ones they tell about the congregation to which they belong may not be authoritative like Scripture, but they are powerful, for they hold the practices that constitute a way of life. Good stories relate not only a plot but also a way of life, just as practices do. Stories, to varying degrees, reveal distilled and illuminated faith revelation. Best to listen to them as we listen to Scripture: pay heed, for this is the word of the Lord.

I am sitting in a room with a woman from the church. The door is open. She whispers, "What I'm about to tell you, I've never told anybody." I hold perfectly still. I don't say a word. "I'm trying to figure out if this is something I can tell others," she says, "or if I need to just keep quiet."

She tells me her story, a rich, dense story full of light and dark and all kinds of in-between nuance. Her story is clear *and* conflicted. The experience she describes has changed her life. God is in the story. It is a sacred story. It has intrinsic value.

I never tell a soul. I wouldn't dare. The story is hers to tell. Besides, she hasn't given me permission to tell others. But the story shapes my ministry. It shapes the life of this congregation. I think about it all the time; while writing a sermon, while moderating a board meeting, while talking to a couple about their wedding, standing over a grave, thinking about the next three years of the congregation. Her story is too holy to be reframed for strategic reasons, captured on video, or even told from the pulpit. But it is powerful.

A thousand of these stories live in any congregation. They reveal key practices. Such stories shape and reshape communal life. Certainly, there are times when such stories can be shared publicly, placed in a sermon or told at a planning meeting. Yet, given the opportunity to live and breathe on their own, such stories have a special, numinous, almost automatic power—the power of God's revelation.

When I left the church I had served for more than fourteen years, a box appeared at the goodbye party. Someone said, "Open it." I looked inside. Amid a stack of notes and pictures was a hat . . . a red hat. Geneva Williams's Sunday hat. The story comes full circle, even as it continues.

Notes

1. Craig Dykstra, *Growing in the Life of Faith: Education and Christian Practices* (Louisville, KY: Geneva Press, 1999), 64.

2. Stephen Crites, "The Narrative Quality of Experience," in *Why Narrative: Readings in Narrative Theology*, ed. Stanley Hauerwas and L. Gregory Jones (Grand Rapids: Eerdmans, 1989), 65–88.

3. Ibid., 81.

4. Anne Tyler, *Saint Maybe* (New York: Ballantine, 1996).

5. Ibid., 118.

6. Ibid., 123.

7. Ibid., 225.

8. Most scholars agree that the verses after Mark 16:8 were added later as a second ending. See Bruce M. Metzger and Bart D. Ehrman, *The Text of the New Testament: Its Transmission, Corruption, and Restoration*, 4th ed. (New York: Oxford University Press, 2005). I am grateful for conversation with William Steele, pastor of the Reformed Church of Bronxville, regarding the connection between the beginning of Mark's Gospel and the abbreviated ending.

9. Robert Kegan, *In Over Our Heads: The Mental Demands of Modern Life* (Cambridge: Harvard University Press, 1994), 355.

10. Dorothy C. Bass, *Practicing Our Faith: A Way of Life for a Searching People* (San Francisco: Jossey-Bass, 1997). This book describes twelve practices. The list is comprehensive, although not necessarily all-inclusive.

11. Marianne Sawicki, *Seeing the Lord: Resurrection and Early Christian Practices* (Minneapolis: Fortress Press, 1994).

12. Ibid., 86–91.

13. Alasdair MacIntyre, *After Virtue*, 2nd ed. (Notre Dame: University of Notre Dame Press, 1984), 188.

14. John S. McClure, *The Roundtable Pulpit: Where Leadership and Preaching Meet* (Nashville: Abingdon Press, 1995).

15. As David brought the Ark of the Covenant to Jerusalem, the oxen carrying the ark stumbled. Uzzah reached out to catch the ark even though God had commanded that the ark not be touched. Punishment for disobedience resulted in Uzzah's death.

CHAPTER 5

Story Sharing and the Practice of Hospitality as Ingredients in Effective Leadership

~

CAROL JOHNSTON

"Carol, we are going to *school* you." And so they would sit me down, these members of Chambers Memorial Baptist Church in East Harlem, and tell me not only stories of their church and their community—stories this young, white seminary student needed to know in order to work in Harlem—but also stories that drew me in, that deepened their welcome of me and wove my life into theirs and their lives into mine. This small, struggling church, located in a neighborhood ravaged by poverty, drugs, and crime, welcomed me and freely shared with me from the deep well of faith and culture that had sustained them for generations of trial.

Looking back, what I remember most vividly, and learned from, were these stories, and the way they made me feel part of the lives of those who told them. Stories of struggles, trials, and triumphs; of powerful adversaries; some white allies; and many foolish white seminary students who learned more from them by far than the students were able to give. Stories told not only with affection and humor and a flair for the dramatic, but also with a keen sense of what was important. Most of all, they were stories of how to act as a Christian through every kind of circumstance. Every Friday night during Advent and Lent they would meet in someone's apartment in "the projects" for a session of B&B—Bottle and Bible study. The first hour would be Bible study. Then the Aretha Franklin records would be played, rum and Coke would be poured, and the storytelling would begin:

"This neighborhood used to be Italian. In the '50s blacks began to move in and most of the Italians moved out. An elderly Italian woman lived across the street from the church, and she resented us. Every Sunday as we went into church, she leaned out of her apartment window and yelled at us—terrible, ugly things. For months and months. Then one Sunday she was not at the window. So we got a group together to go and check on her. When she did not answer her door, we got the super [building superintendent] to go in. Lord, what a mess. She had had a stroke and was lying on the floor in filth from years of neglect and at least twenty cats! We got her to the hospital and then we rolled up our sleeves and cleaned that place from top to bottom."

This story was filled with humorous descriptions of the cats, the mess, and the labor of cleaning up. It ended, as many of their stories did, with a refrain based in their practice of Christian faith: "You don't have to like them, but you do have to love them." For these Christians, doing good to those that hate you and loving your enemies was no abstraction but a concrete aspect of daily life and work.

For them, the love of God made known in Jesus Christ is not just real but also a reality to live and to share with each and every human being. And the best way to share that reality concretely is to practice hospitality—to welcome the stranger with deeds of kindness and to treat everyone, regardless of their behavior toward you, with respect and dignity. More than that, one of the best ways for them to teach this gospel to others is not only to live it but also to share stories of how it works in their lives. After all, human beings have been sharing stories in community for thousands of years, and Jesus understood very well the transforming power of such story sharing. All his teaching was founded on it, and so was the life of the early church. Human beings are wired for stories, and the gospel is above all a story of how God acts through Jesus Christ to restore human beings to right relationships with God, other human beings, and the rest of creation. The right stories bear within them many layers of meaning and insight, and when shared in the right circumstances, they also bear revelatory power.

Hospitality—Genuine, Authentic, Unique

~

Critical to the purposes of the Alban Institute's Narrative Leadership project is understanding not only how this story sharing is integral to the practice of hospitality but also how the practice of hospitality is crucial for effective congregational leadership. In the late 1990s the Lilly Endowment funded a project to study the relation between faith and giving.[1] A key premise of the project was that it would be useful to learn from laity who are actually generous givers, rather than try to do surveys or use other more impersonal forms of data gathering. One by one, dozens of generous church and community leaders in five vitally effective congregations were asked to tell their stories, which were subsequently mined for fresh theological insight— a kind of inductive theological method.[2] The surprise commonality that emerged from the five widely different congregations was not that generosity grew from a theology of stewardship, or preaching about giving and generosity, or teaching pledging and tithing. Not at all. What virtually everyone interviewed talked about over and over was how the church received them with genuine and authentic hospitality that made the love of God actual for them and for each and every human being that came within the congregation's reach. This was at the root of the individuals' generosity, because it was their response to the generosity of God toward them through Jesus Christ and extended concretely by means of the preaching, worship, and welcome practiced in the congregation.

Each congregation practices hospitality differently and uniquely, in accordance with its own theological and ethnic cultures. The Episcopal parish, cognizant of how complicated it is for newcomers to follow the prayer book and hymnal and Bible all at once, but unwilling to simplify their liturgy, prints the entire worship service to make it easier to follow—often filling eighteen pages! The members of the Catholic cathedral in San Antonio, largely Mexican Americans and many extremely poor, take great pride in welcoming visitors to *their* cathedral orally with smiles and words of welcome and making a place for newcomers in the crowded masses. All of them practice hospitality very intentionally as integral to Christian faith, and their leaders encourage everyone to think about ways to practice it in their context and in their own way. In San Antonio one member told me that even though many of them had experienced rejection in European American parishes, they had decided they would never do the same: "God's house has room for *all* his children, and therefore we welcome *everyone* here."

I found among the Mexican American Catholics in San Antonio a particularly strong culture of hospitality and some especially effective ways to practice it. Many homes have a family altar with statues of Jesus, Mary, and various saints and also photos of family members and items with special meaning to the family. When the extended family gathers for special celebrations after a time apart, everyone gathers around the family altar. One by one, each person brings something to place on the altar and explains why it is meaningful to them. In this way, each family member is welcomed back into the home and, by sharing a story of their lives away, is able to contribute something of themselves to the others. This story sharing is a powerful way to knit people together. It includes some elements that are crucial for congregational leaders to understand.

Inviting people to share something of themselves acknowledges that they have a gift to offer to the community. Too much of congregational life is focused on one of two extremes: either trying too hard to show people how the congregation is going to meet their needs or, on the other hand, trying too hard to *get* people involved in the activities of the congregation. Adult education is often based on imparting (in many cases much-needed) knowledge, and too rarely is there time for adult learners to respond to what is being taught and to contribute their insights and views from their own experience. But American culture is rife with loneliness, and one of the greatest needs of any human being is to be known for who he or she is. How many people do we know by name, work with every day, worship with frequently, and yet know very little about? How much of the busyness of life, including life in congregations, is about getting things done and how little is about knitting together human beings in the relational networks that sustain us all? Yet the gospel is about exactly that—restoring right relationships in every part of life, so it is critical for the church to focus on that as central to its life and mission.

Kathleen Norris, in her book *Dakota: A Spiritual Geography*, writes about the hospitality practiced by the Benedictine monks she visits. They understand that Christian hospitality is about much more than welcoming new people into *our* church or even being generous with strangers in order to meet their needs. Too often the first is based on the idea that the church is unchanging and newcomers must fit in. And the second is based on an idea that *we* are rich and *they* are poor, which can slide into condescension and paternalism. The secret of Benedictine hospitality, according to Norris's account, is that they know they need to be open to receive the gift the stranger brings—both for the sake of the stranger and for the sake of the monks, who otherwise would gradually close themselves off from learning and growing.[3] For the truth is, everyone has gifts to share and everyone has needs only others can meet.

According to the Mexican Americans I interviewed, human beings have gifts to share in a way that is integral to being human—and to deny anyone the chance to share his or her gifts is to deny the person's humanity. One young man told of growing up in a rural parish in Texas where his parents wanted him to help out at the church, yet his help was rejected by others at church as unneeded. The motives for the denial are not known, but what is known is that the parents felt rejected—that their son was not even good enough to sweep up after Mass. When the young man discovered San Fernando Cathedral, he was overjoyed to be invited to help out right away—"the way everyone in a family helps out." I heard another story of how a child was told he need not contribute his nickels to a Sunday school collection for the needy because everyone knew his family was poor. By contrast, a highly successful graphics designer told me how exciting it was, as a twelve-year-old in the African American Baptist church where he grew up, to receive a pledge box on the day he was baptized and joined the church: "The pledge box meant you were now an adult and responsible to contribute just like everyone else." Never mind that it might be only nickels.

But this is not just a matter of how wealthy people treat those in need of material assistance. How church leaders treat wealthy people is also important. Another Mexican American I interviewed had grown a Spanish-language advertising company and eventually sold it for 175 million dollars. He sold it because he had discovered that his best gifts—his creative and artistic abilities—were being overwhelmed by the size of the company. At the same time, people no longer asked him to help with projects he enjoyed. Instead, they asked him only to write checks, as if money was all he was good for. They seemed oblivious to the fact that he had a strong network of influential social relations in the community, a wonderful imagination, and other gifts he might have shared with the church to help leverage the impact of its mission. So he sold his company and started over with a small advertising agency. This time they do half their work pro bono so that he can use all his talents for advertising on behalf of people who need it but can't pay. An order of nuns has no idea that his advertising work for them is worth several hundred thousand dollars. He says he loves his work again and feels that "it gives God pleasure when I use all the gifts I have been given."

Inviting People In

What I discovered as I went about asking generous givers to tell me their stories was how powerful an experience it was for the teller. Every human being has a story, and every story is sacred. The seemingly simple act of being asked to tell your story is a powerful act of affirmation—that you are important and your experience has something important that others can learn from. Just that was a transformative experience for those who shared their stories. In most cases, no one had ever asked them to talk about their faith journey—how they got involved with the church and how they learned generosity. The act of reflecting on this helped them bring to consciousness things about themselves and their families and cultures they had never thought about. The process enlarged their own sense of self and helped them experience themselves as anchored in a larger web of life that added depth of meaning and scope to their lives. Everyone, even those with the most wealth and status (including two television producers and a Fortune 500 CEO), thanked me when we finished. Rather than resenting

giving their time, they cherished it. Often the one-hour interview went much longer because they found the experience so
meaningful. This was quite a contrast to the reaction people
have to filling out surveys. Story sharing knits people together
and builds community. The very impersonality of survey in-
struments precludes this. They might convey information, but
they cannot build a relational network.

Because of this, it seems clear that inviting story sharing is,
in and of itself, a powerful way to practice hospitality. Nevertheless, it takes thoughtful and intentional leadership to do it
well. I have seen young pastors get into trouble because they are
trying too hard to prove to the congregation how much they
know and how good they are, while the congregation is often
more anxious to know that their obviously bright young pastor cares about *them* and is willing to learn from them. This
is where the old practice of visiting can become a most useful
tool. Instead of chatting about this and that, or out of anxiety
trying to impress, a new pastor can use pastoral visits as occasions to invite parishioners to share their stories with them—
stories not only of their daily lives but also of the history and
life of the congregation and the wider community. In that way
a pastor can come up to speed more quickly on what the relational dynamics are, how healthy they are, and where the
trouble spots are. They can also, by listening carefully enough
and long enough, find clues in the stories they hear that will
help them lead the congregation out of those trouble spots and
toward a healthier life together.

How the people tell the story of their congregation tells
much, both good and bad, about the health of the community.
The act of story sharing is a sacred act, but not all stories are
honest and truthful. Some stories help perpetuate unhealthy
dynamics and stave off learning the authenticity Christian faith
is supposed to foster. For example, one very common story in
middle-class America is that everyone in the congregation is
successful in work and family life. The assumption is that ca-

reers are on track, divorce is rare, and "the children are all above average," as humorist Garrison Keillor likes to say. Congregational programs take for granted that most adults over thirty are married and have children. Everyone feels an unspoken cultural pressure to make an effort at least to appear as if everything in life is going well.

For many years this was the case at Mount Tabor Missionary Baptist Church in Miami. This upper middle class congregation of successful African American professionals was driven by the American dream of success in every area of life. At the same time, the church was located in an older neighborhood that had gone downhill in the 1960s and '70s, and by the '80s had degenerated into one of the most crack cocaine-ridden places in the world. The members had long since moved out to affluent suburbs, but they continued to be loyal to the church and were troubled by the ring of crack houses, prostitution, and homeless addicts surrounding the old church. Like most Americans, they had no idea what to do with the devastation outside their doors.

In 1989 Mount Tabor called a new pastor, who set out to lead the church in a new direction. He began with small, easy-to-do steps to reach out to the homeless addicts and encourage them to get clean. Initially, some members of the church strongly resisted these efforts, but as they saw hopeless addicts literally being saved in every way that a human being can be saved and heard their stories every week at the altar call, members began to get inspired, and more and more were drawn to help out. Today Mount Tabor has ministries dealing with every aspect of addictions, and while it ministers effectively to and with the most hopeless, it has remained largely upper middle class and tripled in membership. Visiting their ministries and seeing the contrast between those still using drugs and those in recovery is a remarkable experience. But even more remarkable is the transformation of the members. Along the way, they discovered that addicts can't get clean until they get honest about their addictions, and the members learned they could not help addicts until they learned to get honest about their own lives— their own less-than-perfect families and jobs and their own struggles with divorce and drug abuse and problems at work. What a relief it was to drop the pretense of being ideal families and share the truth about the struggles of their lives. At Mount Tabor, no one needs to pretend anymore, and the energy released by this openness and authenticity is tremendous.

Part of the art of congregational leadership is to know how to encourage people to share their stories, to acknowledge the validity of each point of view, and yet at the same time to encourage people to find the courage to hear stories different from the ones they are used to and to begin to tell stories that are more authentic. Asking people who are respected by others to share their stories is tremendously important—to identify the recognized saints of the congregation and find settings in which they can tell less practiced and less wise members how they go about living out the gospel. For example, in my own experience, I was never taught (in church or in seminary) how or why it is important to be a consistent giver—and never thought about it much—until I moved and attended the new member class of a new congregation. In one of the sessions, a church elder came in, an older businessman, and told us his story of how his family goes about practicing generosity in relation to church giving. His story was riveting, full of humor and insight and a sense of the joy that comes from giving. Learning that giving can be a transforming spiritual practice rather than a disagreeable if necessary obligation was a revelation to me. If a clergyperson had lectured to us that giving can be such an experience, it would have washed right by me, and I daresay by everyone else. But the story shared by someone who was *like those in the class*—someone most of the new members aspired to be like in their careers and family life—was far more powerful and convincing than any lecture could have been.

Thirty years ago, speaking openly about having cancer was taboo in American culture. Cancer patients too often suffered in silence and loneliness, full of fear and feeling abandoned. To change the culture took many courageous people speaking up and telling their own stories of struggling with the disease so that today cancer patients can expect more care from family and friends and less isolation. Another still powerful taboo is speaking out about the reality of domestic violence. A disturbingly large percentage of women and children are victims of domestic violence at some time in their lives, but the expectation is that this reality is not something that happens to the loving families that attend our churches. This false narrative is still doing tremendous damage. But how to address it? A recital of all the statistics usually is either overpowering or dismissed as "not us." But when a respected member of the church, a woman who to all appearances is the epitome of what most members aspire to be like—successful in work, well dressed and physically fit, with a loving husband and children—gets up in church and talks about how her first husband beat her and threatened her life and the lives of her children, then people pay attention. Once again, the story is all the more convincing and transformative because someone the people identify with is telling it. And this, too, is part of the practice of Christian hospitality, because it is part of welcoming everyone to participate in the transformative power of authentic narrative.

Setting Direction

Clearly, not just any story will do. It is too easy for story sharing to degenerate into storytelling for the sake of storytelling, with no sense of direction and no insight or meaning to it. When a group gets uncomfortable and anxious, people may be tempted to dodge hard thinking and truth telling by sliding off into mere storytelling. Yes, the energy level immediately rises, and the sense of relief is palpable. Sometimes this is necessary. People can take only so much anxiety. Theologian Robert McAfee Brown used to describe how good narrative—what we might call today narrative leadership—helps draw people beyond their comfort zones, but not so far that they dig in and resist and then refuse to come along at all. You can't use narratives that are too alien to the people you are working with and require them to take too big a leap. And yet you have to resist the temptation to settle for only the safe narratives.

That is why asking the members to tell their own stories is so important, to share their memories of the congregation and even to dig up long-past history. It is often the case that some memory, some counternarrative is healthier than where the congregation is now. This alternate story can be retrieved and drawn on to help people reframe their congregational sense of self and sense of what is possible for them as a community as well as individuals. If it is something *we* used to do, then it is somehow more acceptable to do it again. When the Catholic cathedral in Louisville discovered that the hungry had been fed on that site since the 1830s—since before there *was* a cathedral—that history was told over and over, and the practice of handing out baloney sandwiches to the homeless became a matter of historical pride instead of a sore point.

Stories also work more effectively when asking people to understand the point of view of those who are perceived as different and "other"—if the difference can be overcome by the shared humanity conveyed through the testimony of the teller. The reason is that human beings naturally identify with the subjects in stories, and stories can elicit human sympathy in a way that nothing else can. It is no accident that the TV miniseries *Roots* was experienced as a watershed in U.S. race relations. The story of Kunta Kinte was told in such a way that, for the first time, large numbers of white Americans were drawn to identify with the experience of an African who was captured, endured the terrible Middle Passage to America, was sold into slavery, attempted escape, and struggled his whole life to hang on to the memory of who he was and where he came from and to pass that memory down through the generations of his descendants in America. The story was so powerful that it spawned a new passion among European- and African-descended Americans alike to learn the stories of their own families. And above all, the story helped white America begin to understand black experience in a new, more personally felt way. Similarly, the mission work of congregations has always been most effectively fostered by the stories told by those who have visited the places where mission work is going on and can testify from firsthand experience as to what is happening there.

Sometimes the seemingly simple act of feeling *heard* is enough to change the behavior of people in the midst of controversy. A growing United Methodist congregation was trying to decide whether to move or to stay, which would require renovating and adding to their existing building. The committee selected to study the matter recommended the congregation stay and build a large new sanctuary, but many people resisted fiercely. In order to try to work through the ensuing conflict, the pastor asked members for and against to pair off. Each had to listen to the other explain their reasons and then say the reasons back to his or her partner well enough that the other person agreed that his or her views were being fairly stated. That simple exercise, in which each person was asked to listen hospitably to the views of an opponent, changed the whole process. Those who objected felt heard, and most eventually dropped their opposition—enough to allow the new building to be built with strong support.

Not all stories are theologically equal. What separates good sermon stories from mediocre ones is the way the stories actually convey real theological insight related to the truth being told, rather than simply providing a bit of relief when the sermon starts to drag. Communicating real insight takes thoughtfulness, disciplined study, and an imaginative eye for the right stories for any given context. It helps a great deal to keep the matter of right relationships in view and to look for ways to correlate stories with particular issues and needs. The good news is that the Bible is full of stories of the endless ways relationships are broken and restored, and so the standard of Christian faith and life is also the source of endlessly helpful narratives.

I experienced an example of how this can work the first time I was asked to lead an adult study group on faith and economics. A group made up largely of corporate executives from Rancho Palos Verdes, California, invited me to lead them in a study of the U.S. Catholic bishops' letter on economics, which had recently been published. I soon realized that the letter was much more liberal than the group, and so was I. The temptation to browbeat them with the letter's left-wing views was strong, but I knew that if I did so they would simply dismiss me and the letter both. Also, Christian hospitality in my mind meant respecting them and their views as well as asking them to respect those of the letter. So instead of lecturing at them, I invited them to wrestle with the views in the letter as honestly and authentically as they could, and I led them through that without giving them my own views. I also began the class by inviting them to discuss the section of the letter about the vocation of the laity and relate it to their own sense of vocation. No one had ever invited any of them to share stories about their sense of vocation in their work lives before. The story sharing made the collection of individuals into a much more closely connected group. And to my surprise, I also soon discovered that they were more than willing to wrestle honestly and were genuinely troubled by much of what they experienced in the business world, in contradiction to my own prejudices about what conservative business executives would think. Nevertheless, when we came to the letter's affirmation that God has a "preferential option for the poor," they did squirm. A lot. I tried to understand their point of view and found myself drawing on the New Testament story of the prodigal son. I asked, "You feel like the older brother in the story of the prodigal son, don't you? You have worked hard all your life and done what you were supposed to, and now the bishops are telling you that God loves the poor more than you, despite all your hard work." They readily agreed with this, and it helped them process their reaction. Then a few weeks later, after we had looked at global resource use and learned about the way the United States uses energy and resources at a vastly greater rate than any other nation, even those wealthier than we, I brought them back to the prodigal son story: "If we take a long-run, global view of this story, who is squandering the inheritance now? The poor in the developing world or the United States?" I did not have to give the answer. But I did have to remind them that the story is about the patience of the father who waits for both sons to realize that right relationships, loving relationships are more important than who gets what and to recognize who steadfastly welcomed both despite their erring ways.

Since that class, I have been convinced that it is more effective, more theologically sound—in short, more hospitable—to refrain from making assumptions about where people are and to invite people to wrestle honestly with whatever the topic is, rather than to try to convince them of a particular point of view. I encourage them to share their stories of where they are and why they think the way they do, then I connect that with biblical and other stories that have some fresh insight or wisdom to offer in the specific context. Next I ask for reactions to it, which give me more ideas for moving the discussion forward, as well as insights I had not thought of, receiving the gifts those learning with me have to bring.

People may not be where I want them to be, but if they are moving in the right direction (for them, not necessarily in what I think is the best way), and if I trust that the Holy Spirit is at work in the process and I stay out of the way, I am often surprised at how far they go—far beyond what they and I initially thought was possible. I should not be surprised—the same thing happened to me on my own journey into faith. And I do think there is such a thing as a right direction for practicing Christian faith. It is possible to see at work in people a transformational trajectory that includes such matters as moving from fear to trust, from hiding to authenticity, from brokenness to healing, from anxiety to security, from avarice to generosity, from aggressiveness to authentic self-confidence, and the like.

Making Safe Space

Stories that illustrate this transformational trajectory are the most effective kind to share, but they can also be the scariest because they reveal our vulnerabilities and shortcomings. Consequently, it is of utmost importance to be careful of when and how people are asked to share such stories. People have to feel welcome and safe, and a shared commitment to each other has to be built. I have been in meetings in which those present were told much too soon, "This is a safe place, and you can feel free to say what you really think." The reality was, rather, that most present knew quite well it was not a safe place, and the credibility of the leaders of the program was completely lost because they did not acknowledge that reality. On the other hand, when the leaders of a gathering that has to face difficult issues and conflict not only acknowledge that reality honestly but also are able to draw on a shared sense of belonging, then a much more solid basis for truth telling is laid. When the Episcopal parish in Pasadena gathered in a forum to debate a contentious political issue, the rector reminded everyone that "We are all brothers and sisters in Christ, and therefore stuck with each other—Republicans *and* Democrats alike." Everyone laughed heartily, but most also listened and took the reminder seriously so that the congregation could disagree vehemently and yet also stay together.

Even so, not all gatherings feel hospitable to everyone, and no one in any setting should feel coerced into talking before they are ready. Much more effective is to ask, "Who is ready to go next?" when sharing stories, rather than going around the room. And it is important not to pressure anyone. Nelle Morton, in her book *The Journey Is Home*, relates the experience of a consciousness-raising group of women. Each time they met, they shared more and more of their lives with each other. Yet one of the women never said a word. No one pressured her, and finally on the last day she began, with much hesitation, to talk. What she had to say was painful, but no one rushed her or tried to comfort her. "We simply sat. We sat in a powerful silence. . . . Finally the woman finished speaking. Tears flowed from her eyes in all directions. She spoke again: 'You heard me. You heard me all the way. . . . I have a strange feeling you heard me before I started. You heard me to my own story. *You heard me to my own speech.*'"[4]

Manifesting the Spirit

~

If narrative leadership is about finding stories to tell, stories that help convey what the leaders believe is important or, worse, are used to manipulate or get people to do what congregational leaders have decided for them is what they should do, then the most important part of what is liberating and transformational about story sharing is missed altogether. Congregational leaders, especially Protestant leaders, have been steeped in the Reformation celebration of the word of God preached and taught. The laity are supposed to listen while the leaders proclaim the word. Protestants were so excited about the reforms that made it possible to hear and read God's word in the vernacular that they spent centuries emphasizing the preached word above all else. But preachers are not the only ones who have learned to live the faith with wisdom and insight. Everyone, preachers and parishioners alike, has much to learn from thoughtful saints and loving fools and the struggle of even the most ordinary soul to speak out of their own perception of God's work in their lives and in their struggles to live more faithfully. Yes, everyone needs to learn the word of God in Scripture study, to hear preaching and lectures, and to listen for God's word and will through the practice of prayer. But the appropriation and living out of the faith is a shared enterprise and an active one worked out in the rush of daily life. As the apostle Paul put it so eloquently in his letter to the church at Corinth, "To each is given the manifestation of the Spirit for the common good" (1 Cor. 12:7). When each person is welcomed with true openness to the particular "manifestation of the Spirit" that he or she bears and is encouraged to share the sacred stories of how the faith is understood and practiced, then the whole body is enriched and lives are transformed for the sake of reconciling the world.

Notes

1. The grant project was called "Thinking Theologically about Faith, Wealth, and Community Leadership," Christian Theological Seminary, Indianapolis, IN, 1996.

2. The congregations were All Saints Episcopal, Pasadena, CA; San Fernando Catholic Cathedral, San Antonio, TX; Catholic Cathedral of the Assumption, Louisville, KY; Mount Tabor Missionary Baptist Church, Miami, FL; and Fifth Avenue Presbyterian Church, New York.

3. Kathleen Norris, *Dakota: A Spiritual Geography* (New York: Houghton Mifflin, 1993).

4. Nelle Morton, *The Journey Is Home* (Boston: Beacon Press, 1985), 204–5.

CHAPTER 6

Have Conversations
and Have Faith

TRADING "US AND THEM" FOR "ALL OF US"

~

MIKE MATHER

In Acts 2, Peter stands in the streets and quotes from the prophet Joel, telling the crowd that God's Spirit flows down upon all people—women and men, young and old. That remarkable event reminds us of the unity *and* the universality of God's gift to the world. Also significant is the fact that at that first Pentecost, members of the crowd heard in their own language what Peter proclaimed. The gift of the Spirit was one known both in the moment of hearing and in the way that the early Christian community then acted on what they heard. The Pentecost story is one in a long line of narratives that remind us that the biblical story is *our* story, and that it is the story of both the church and the world.

The chapel at Broadway United Methodist Church in Indianapolis, where I serve as pastor, has a beautiful stained glass window depicting John Wesley, the founder of Methodism. The quote beneath his image reads, "I look upon all the world as my parish." Every Sunday morning when I see that window I am reminded that we at Broadway are not limited to the exclusive belief that "the church is our parish." Instead, we want to recognize all the ways in which God is already dancing in the lives of our neighbors. We know that if we don't pay attention to what God is doing around us, we will all end up poorer for it.

As an urban church in a low-income neighborhood, we do not have the luxury of looking at our parish through the eyes of a glorious past and ignoring our world today. The days when thousands of people filled our pews are only a part of Broadway's history. Today we have to depend on an abundance of gifts instead of an abundance of people. At times we can easily feel poor ourselves, as many other churches do. Yet the truth is, just as we are surrounded by a great cloud of witnesses from the past, God still surrounds us with an abundance of gifts today. We need to remind ourselves of that all the time. One way to do so is to look for gifts in unexpected places: among the poor, in our low-income neighborhood, and among those we have yet to meet.

Four years ago I came back to Broadway after being away for more than eleven years. When I returned, the congregation held a series of gatherings to give me and the members a chance to meet and listen to one another. As these gatherings proceeded, I began to notice that I was hearing the same things over and over again. I was hearing people talk about the gifts that filled the congregation as well as their dreams for the congregation and the surrounding community. I was impressed with the clarity they had in naming what they felt God was calling us to do in the areas of music, economic development, care of the building, children and youth, and local and global mission. Our challenge, however, was to find solid ways of accomplishing our dreams. Although we had clear ideas about what we wanted to do in the areas mentioned above, we had unrealistic ideas of how we could accomplish them. The challenge was to figure out how to do what we felt God was calling us to do.

As a first step toward tackling that challenge, a few church leaders—both clergy and lay—embarked on a period of discernment. This led us to the conclusion that we needed to dramatically expand and reconfigure our staff to give these dreams a chance to become real, make our dreams a reality. When we met to share our conclusions with the congregation, one member responded excitedly, "It's been a long time since we've had a dreamer for a pastor." This concerned me. "No," I said. "If you think these are my dreams, we need to get up and walk away from this. If these aren't your dreams, let's stop this right now." I went on to point out that the congregation had always had dreamers. "They sit next to you in the pews. They are your neighbors. The dreamers aren't the pastors. The dreamers are you. I trust the Spirit of God working in and through you." Over the next year, we asked ourselves two questions: "Is this where God is calling us as a congregation?" and "Is it doable?" The people thought about it, talked about it, and prayed about it. It became clear that adding staff in order to support these dreams was one way of investing in what God is doing around us and in the dreams of the people of our parish. We began to restructure ourselves by building on the gifts of the people in our congregation, continuing to ask ourselves, "Is this where God is calling us, and is it doable?"

At the heart of the changes we were making was the re-imagining of our Nominating Committee in a way that could better serve this new vision. We renamed that group the Committee on Lay Leadership to embrace the new task of having conversations with people in and around the life of the church, including nonmembers. Now the committee pays attention to what its members see as people's gifts and sense of God's call and claim upon their lives. Then the congregation tries to discern ways that we, as the body of Christ, can encourage and build one another up in those callings. The committee sees if there are people inside and around the congregation who we can bring together to connect around their calls.

In addition to being intentional about discerning the gifts of people in the congregation, its leaders, lay and clergy, also felt we needed to be intentional about discerning the gifts of our neighbors. It was important to us to adopt the wider sense of parish that is part of our Wesleyan heritage. Why? First, we knew that as a congregation we could easily grow too insular and think ministry is all about us. We could pull in upon ourselves and provide comfort and care only for those inside our walls. Second, we realized we might develop a bunker mentality of "us versus them," which would prevent us from growing our dreams and what God is already doing in and around us. We wanted to erase the notions of *us* and *them* until everyone was part of *us*.

Looking Beyond Needs

A short time after initiating Broadway's plan to realize our vision, our lay and clergy leaders were in conversation with representatives of the local neighborhood development corporation (the city's housing program) as they were preparing to go through a strategic planning process to determine how they could best serve the community. A key part of their plan was to do a needs survey in the community. This bothered us.

The data resulting from so-called needs surveys are the most popular tools driving strategic planning in community institutions and associations of all types. Over the past fifteen years I have been asked time and again to contribute to needs surveys organized by local hospitals, universities, Boys and Girls Clubs, YMCAs, and especially the United Way. All of these groups want to know what we in the city are lacking, what is wrong with us. They don't seem very interested in what is right with us. This makes us wonder who has the real need here. Perhaps these organizations *need* to know what is wrong with us more than what is right with us. They don't seem to need or want what we have to offer.

As a vivid example, the urban neighborhood of another congregation I served (in another city) was selected as a site for the "Christmas in April" program that renovates homes in low-income communities. The good people who were leading this program invited the pastors and a few other community leaders to a meeting six months prior to the work day. We expected them to ask us for volunteers from our congregations and community who had gifts to give to this effort. But they didn't want that. Instead, they encouraged us to convince our neighbors that the volunteers' work was a good thing, because, as one representative told us, "Sometimes we are seen as an invading army and that causes problems." When we asked about volunteers from the community, they replied, "We don't need any of your people." Apparently, the only thing they needed was our neediness—our emptiness, our poverty—to fulfill their mission. How sad.

Now the neighborhood's development corporation was speaking to us in the same vein. Theologically, we had problems with this approach because it failed to recognize our neighbors as beloved children of God who had gifts to offer that we would be poorer without. Strategically, we had problems with the plan as well, because across the years there had been so little to show for shaping programs around needs. In fact, one could argue that despite all the work of community agencies to serve so-called needs, things have actually become worse.

So, both theologically and practically, we encouraged the development corporation to build its strategic plan for the surrounding parish on the gifts of our neighbors and trust that in that process the community's needs would be met. We held firmly to this notion, reminding ourselves of the stories Jesus told about mustard seeds and a single treasure buried in a field. And we reminded ourselves of Jesus feeding the multitudes and the abundance gathered afterward, when the disciples had been eager to send the "needy" crowd away.

Knowing Our Neighbor

~

We ultimately formed a partnership with the development corporation and, with support from the Indianapolis Center for Congregations, created a position we called the Roving Listener. We hired a talented young man—De'Amon Harges, a church member and neighborhood resident—to go through the neighborhood and talk with everyone he met. He was to talk with old folks and young, women and men. He was to listen for their gifts, their dreams, and their sense of God's call and claim upon their lives. De'Amon knew that you couldn't simply ask people what their gifts and dreams were and expect an honest answer. (Many of us have a hard time discerning for ourselves what our gifts are, or perhaps we are too humble to put ourselves and our gifts forward.) So he paid attention to what people said about one another. He asked people what they thought others' gifts were. He asked parents to speak about their children, and children to speak about their parents. He asked neighbor to speak about neighbor. And he listened with both his ears and his eyes, paying attention to people's expressions and energy as they spoke: When did they really light up? When did they laugh? He paid attention to how people truly revealed who they were and what they had to offer.

De'Amon's role for the development corporation was to supply them with information about the gifts of the neighborhood's residents—their interests, callings, and passions. De'Amon and his friend and advisor Mike Green say that they are looking for "what people care enough about to actually get up off the couch and do." That is something distinctly different than what someone has an opinion about. The congregation was interested in doing something that actually works for people rather than something that we think *ought* to work or that we think *someone* should do.

In low-income communities like ours (as in most communities), there are as many needs as there are stars in the sky. Trying to do something about all of them will only end up overwhelming and overpowering everyone. Instead, at Broadway we believe that if we do the parts we are called to do, however many or few those may be, it will not only be enough, it will be more than enough. We really do believe that "our cup runneth over."

The development corporation, under the inspired leadership of its director, Shary Johnston, decided to go about their work in a unique way. They decided *not* to do a needs survey based on perceived deficits but instead to use the data provided by our Roving Listener to build their strategic plan on the gifts of our neighbors. The corporation continues to grapple with how to use that good information, as does the church.

Broadway decided to use De'Amon's findings more individually—person by person. We took the information he was discovering and tried to find ways to build upon it. At the Committee on Lay Leadership, we shared his findings, sometimes even inviting people De'Amon had talked with to participate in our meetings. Many questions arose for us as we gathered: How could we begin to act on what we have heard? Should we develop a database of the many and varied gifts we had learned about? How would we know that our response to what we were learning was what we were supposed to be doing?

Around that time De'Amon said something that has resonated through our halls ever since: "Have conversations and have faith!" Many times, in meetings or conversations where we are trying to figure out what to do next, someone is bound to say, "Have conversations and have faith."

About six months after De'Amon started doing this work, we invited all the people he had talked with thus far to attend a luncheon being held at the church. More than a third of them came. De'Amon seated people together based on their interests, and this great and glad gathering was unlike any I had ever seen at a church. It was a gathering of those who are considered the poor and those who aren't, of those who live in "bad neighborhoods" and those who don't. However, the focus was not on misery or needs or services supplied. Instead, the luncheon was a chance for people who care about the same things simply to get together and enjoy each other.

Out of that luncheon relationships began to form. People asked whether we had an agenda for something to come from this, but our genuine intention was to simply "have conversations and have faith." And that is what we did, continually asking ourselves how we could build on the gifts of the Spirit in our midst.

One step we took on this journey was to look at the conversations De'Amon had in the neighborhoods, and we began to see some patterns emerging. We began to witness three categories of people's gifts—economic development, health, and the arts—woven in and through a large portion of those conversations, so we asked our two interns from Christian Theological Seminary in Indianapolis to gather people from these interest groups for a meal and watch what developed. I can tell you that the interns were more than a little bit confused at first. "But what are we supposed to do?" they asked. "Just get these folks who care about the same thing together and stand back and watch," we told them. During those meals, people came together and discovered the joy of talking with others who care about the same thing. We ultimately sponsored dinner or evening conversations with an artists' group, a health group, a legal group, a gardening group, and a cooks' group. We supported these groups by giving them opportunities to take trips to visit others who were doing interesting work in the same arena. We also provided them with some books in their area of interest. And we brought in people involved in these interest areas to come and talk with them.

Soon some of these groups began to plan and to act. For example, a couple of doctors in the congregation offered to get more than one hundred blood-pressure cuffs for members of the health group to use to take the blood pressures of their neighbors. We did this *not* primarily to improve the health of our neighbors but to improve connections between neighbors—which we believe will result in better health. Later we decided to hire people from the neighborhood who De'Amon had discovered had gifts for organizing in the interest areas we had identified. Each of these people is now responsible for working with other interested people and is encouraged to build on his or her own connections as well. Out of this process, we believe we are building awareness in people's hearts of the Spirit's presence in their lives and in their world. Some people call this empowerment, but we don't. *Empowerment* is a word meaning "to give power to" people, but we are not doing that at all. What we are doing is recognizing God's power already at work in the gifts of the people of our parish and finding ways to invest in that power for strengthening the community.

One story in particular serves to illustrate how this can happen. For more than thirty years our congregation has had a tutoring ministry. It has even been recognized by the mayor as a particularly shining example of what can and should be done by congregations involved in their communities. It has involved volunteers from the congregation, from other congregations (outside the neighborhood), and from businesses, but we have never really looked for tutors from around the neighborhood. Now perhaps that doesn't seem strange, but it should. Certainly any neighborhood has varieties of people with varieties of gifts. And why shouldn't a low-income neighborhood have people who can and should tutor?

As De'Amon visited around the neighborhood, he met Maya Neely, a young woman who was running a tutoring program out of her house, just a few blocks away from the church! I called her. "What do you teach?" I asked. "Everything from phonics to Sophocles," she told me. What a joy it was to talk with her. She would invite her neighbors to come and work with her, give them reading and writing assignments, then she would have the children share what they had written. What a gift she is offering. What was happening at the church wasn't bad; we simply needed to widen the scope of what we were doing. What we are *also* called to do is to find ways to build up, join, and strengthen what neighbors like Maya are doing. Is that not a *charism*, a gift of the Spirit itself? Of course it is. What Maya is doing is as much a call from God as anything done within the walls of our church building.

I have come to believe that the kind of questions the church asks gives us the answers we find. On the one hand, if we want to know how to meet needs, we can do that and those needs may well be met. But meeting needs doesn't get us all that we are truly seeking. Do we really want to give someone a few groceries to last for just three days? Or do we want to have the chance to involve ourselves in the gifts of the person who comes seeking that food, gifts that we will be poorer without? In the process, we may find out that the person's food needs get taken care of in another way, for the long haul. This is not about "teaching people to fish," as some would say, but about something much more.

On the other hand, if the church wants to invest in the gifts of the Spirit already present in the lives of people, then we must start by having conversations with them. How will we discover what the calling and claim of God upon our lives is until we listen to and see what God is doing in the lives of our sisters and brothers? If we limit our vision to what is inside "the church," we will be blind to what is happening in the amazing world around us. Instead of focusing on one small area of God's activity, we need to draw attention to God's activity in all the world around us. When we do so, we are able to share one of the unique gifts we have with the world: listening to and celebrating people's God-given gifts.

Around the time of Broadway's restructuring, we began a new liturgical practice that weaves together our worship and our new structure. Once a month in worship, right before the final hymn, we celebrate ministries that have died, ministries that are continuing, and ministries that are beginning. Honoring what has died helps us to acknowledge things that have been done and that have shaped us across the years but that we are no longer called to continue. When we name and celebrate a ministry that has ended, we ask all those who have supported it across the years to stand and be recognized. And then the congregation says to them, together, "Well done, good and faithful servants." We then celebrate a continuing ministry, and we recognize and honor those who have and are continuing to support that ministry. When we recognize the new ministries, we have fun recognizing and acknowledging the Spirit at work in new ways, not only among our congregation but also outside our walls, as we did with Maya and the tutoring ministry.

Maya came to worship one Sunday to be recognized as a new ministry of Broadway. Her ministry was not new to her, of course, but it was new to our awareness. Maya, who was sitting in the front row, stood when we asked those involved in this ministry to stand. We then asked those who were willing to support this ministry with their prayers, their presence, their gifts, or their service to stand. Maya didn't realize that the whole congregation was now standing behind her. "Will you do everything in your power to uphold and care for this person in her ministry?" the congregation was asked. When they thundered, "We will!" Maya jumped and turned around with joy and surprise.

We have discovered that new things are going on all the time. Or, more precisely, we are becoming more and more aware of what is going on around us all the time!

This journey of the body of Christ at Broadway has deepened my own faith. It has helped me to connect to the stories of Jesus curing people of blindness—blindness to their own gifts and to those of people around them. Now I understand why. One of the real obstacles to recognizing the abundance around us is the sense in mainstream U.S. Protestantism that ministry is only what happens in and through the agency of the church. On the contrary, congregations are full of people, gifted people, committed people, who have ministries—in their homes, their workplaces, their businesses, their schools, and with others (with friends, with those who are ill, with those who suffer)—and yet so many of them don't think of what they do as ministry. How has our language and our practice gone so far off course? Because of these inherited assumptions, we in the church sometimes struggle with what to do with the information the Roving Listener is uncovering. We know what to do if someone wants to volunteer in one of our programs, but how do we invest in the Spirit's labor in others' lives? What we at Broadway keep learning, or keep trying to remind ourselves of, is that it is not that hard, really. It means we need to stay focused on having more conversations and having faith.

One of the things we have discovered along the way is that when we recognize one another as beloved children of God with something to offer for the building up of the community and God's world, we really do all end up richer for it, and there is real joy in it. It is hard work (it is difficult to look at things with new eyes), but the joy is never ceasing as we walk together down God's broad way.

CHAPTER 7

Downtown Judaism—
in Our Own Image

~

NILES ELLIOT GOLDSTEIN

About a week after the collapse of the World Trade Center on 9/11, I walked through Ground Zero. It was during the Days of Awe. Before me was utter devastation: a wasteland of smashed buildings and shattered windows; hideous, fantastic pillars of twisted steel; plumes of smoke rising eerily from the rubble.

As a law enforcement chaplain, I talked to cops, agents, fire-fighters, and rescue workers from dozens of agencies and cities. I remember one K-9 unit, a sheriff's deputy and his dog. Even though by that point all they were pulling out were bodies, his Labrador retriever wouldn't let him sleep. Everyone there, whether human or animal, was focused on their work, on trying to serve.

I was moved by the acts of commitment and expressions of love that permeated that hellish place. And I was astounded by the vision of so many people finding their deepest, most beautiful selves in the heart of such an immense void.

That experience was mirrored when my congregation, The New Shul, held our Rosh Hashanah services in Greenwich Village only a few blocks north of the terrorist attack. Several of our households had suddenly become homeless and were living out of luggage. Our children were stunned and scared, many having witnessed with their own eyes men and women leaping to their deaths onto the streets in front of them. Our adult members clung to their cell phones tightly, as if they were guard rails, waiting anxiously to hear news about missing friends, colleagues, and family.

I had torn up my sermons days before. What we did instead was share our collective feelings and thoughts. People spoke, embraced one another, and wept.

Yet no one was alone.

As downtown Manhattan's youngest synagogue, we had been in existence at that point for only a couple of years, but the fact that we had created a community—and a *sanctuary*, a true safe haven—for those who now so desperately craved one was as palpable as it was profound. I felt a sense of intense pride in what we had accomplished in such a relatively brief period of time.

After the horrors of 9/11, lower Manhattan began to undergo great change, development, and growth—and that applied to the Jewish community, too.

Those who had been made homeless by homicidal Islamic extremists gradually began to return to their damaged homes. As new high-rise residential buildings started to go up, Jews from around the city began to move down from other areas. With more Jews now in need of more Jewish activities and communities, there was a slow but steady increase in Jewish life and institutions below Fourteenth Street, as well as a vitality and dynamism that I had rarely seen in my years of working as a New York rabbi.

In close parallel with our own philosophy when we founded The New Shul pre-9/11, most of these *post*-9/11 initiatives strived to reflect both the creativity and the sensibility of the Jews who were attracted to these neighborhoods.

High-profile Jewish arts and culture festivals started drawing large crowds and taking place in unusual venues:

Tribeca Hebrew created a new religious school that ran in the basement of a storefront; the Soho Synagogue, a Chabad-led congregation, threw lavish Kabbalat Shabbat cocktail parties; the Fourteenth Street Y, under the auspices of the venerable Educational Alliance, worked to reinvent itself as an outpost of East Village hipness; the Downtown Kehillah, a multidenominational consortium of downtown synagogues, tried to build bridges between communities; and the Jewish Community Project, a self-styled alternative version of the Ninety-Second Street Y, emerged out of this same impulse and energy.

Balancing Tradition and Innovation

A few years have now passed. And with the shift in downtown demographics, a marked shift in mindset is also evident.

Most of the initiatives above share certain traits, characteristics that we had already deliberately lined into the fabric of our own community years before: a "come as you are" attitude, with a focus on inclusivity for all, regardless of belief or background; a grassroots, egalitarian approach to Jewish life; a decentralized leadership structure; a tendency toward non- or postdenominational Judaism; multiple and diverse paths for expressing Jewish identity; an eclecticism in vision and in mission.

At the core of all of this, of course, was a general disaffection with, and a detachment from, the Jewish status quo.

Why else build something new?

These new Jewish institutions and initiatives have made some of the founding members of my community (and, to be frank, myself) feel a bit like grizzled pioneers—a very strange sensation for a young congregation like ours. But they have also made us feel that we are not alone in craving a new kind of Jewish community, one that more closely reflects the kinds of Jews we actually are—and that we want to be.

Yet, in my view, new problems have slowly, inexorably emerged. As a rabbi who has witnessed the changes in Jewish life in lower Manhattan both before and after 9/11, I have the privilege of a unique and firsthand perspective. Working here in the trenches, I have to say that I do not like everything that I have seen.

Committed is not a word I would use to describe the typical downtown Jew in this post-9/11 world. We want some form of Jewish life, but we want it on our own terms, at times when it is convenient for us, and in small, easy-to-swallow doses. We don't want a lot of expectations placed on us. We want to be entertained, not challenged. We want, as one person once put it to me, "just the fun stuff," without any of the communal responsibility our religion associates with being a member of the Jewish people. We are not into the serious exploration of Jewish traditions and texts, but we (and our leaders) are preoccupied with, almost obsessed by, the idea of edginess.

Moreover, our new efforts are beginning to fall prey to age-old problems: territorialism, politics, replication of one another, a lack of unity.

As someone who has served downtown Jews for nearly a decade, I am certain that we must remain as vigilant as ever, but in radically new ways. Anti-Semitism, intermarriage, and assimilation are not my biggest concerns.

My biggest worry is vapidity.

When viewed through the lens of history, Jews have always been engaged in the process of reshaping Judaism and Jewish life in our own image. So let's make sure that image is one that remains creative and dynamic, but let's also stay true to our tradition's bold, countercultural roots—the roots that have made us who we are.

The Bible teaches us that there may very well be a time for all things under the sun, but now is certainly *not* the time to embrace the widespread narcissism, materialism, and "You better give me what I want or I just won't show up" sense of entitlement that is so much a part of American (and of Jewish American) culture these days.

Now is the time to fight those trends with all our heart, soul, and being.

The Search for Community

I have written about my own experiences and observations about the role that religion and religious life can and have played in our post-9/11 world. Although, as a rabbi, I have written from a specifically Jewish vantage point, most of the reactions and responses I have witnessed (both in New York City and on my speaking engagements around the United States and among other faith traditions) reach across the spectrum of American religious life, and have far-reaching and important implications for our congregational leaders—both clerical and lay—and our spiritual institutions.

One thing that has become crystal clear to me is that men and women are looking for *communities*, not congregations. Most people care very little about denominational labels or theology. Some don't even care about the institution of religion itself (I know some individuals who actually belong to two or more different congregations of different faiths and move with ease between their respective worship services and programs).

The icons, symbols, and images of the past no longer hold power for this new generation of Americans. Some of the largest and most dynamic megachurches, for example, do not even have crosses in their facilities, let alone fixed pews or pulpits. What people seem to crave is a sense of community, a feeling of being wanted and known.

Ultimately, we want to be loved, and to find protection through that love.

I believe that we need to rethink our congregations today less as houses of worship than as *sanctuaries* in the true, etymological meaning of the word—a place of safety and security. These are troubling times, and offering Americans a safe haven amidst the maelstrom around us is a very appealing gift. A sanctuary is different from a church or a synagogue. A sanctuary is not about symbols, rituals, sacred texts, or holy days—it is more about, as the Jewish evening liturgy states, being "guarded under the shelter of Your wings." We have a military to guard our bodies. Who will protect our souls?

If we can transform congregations into sanctuaries and safe havens, we can begin to offer the shelter that so many people yearn for but cannot seem to find. But then new questions will arise that we must confront:

+ With less emphasis on prayer, study, and theology, and more on interpersonal connection and inclusivity, what is it exactly that our spiritual institutions stand for?
+ Are we simply giving the people what they want, or are we holding fast to age-old values and principles?
+ Is it possible to strike the proper balance between creating innovative projects and initiatives and conserving the traditional pillars of our rich and ancient faiths?

These are difficult questions that are appropriate for these difficult times. In an age of shocking religious extremism, how do we as religious leaders present our respective faith traditions as relevant, meaningful, purpose driven, even edgy?

Is Leadership a
Four-Letter Word Today?

⌒

There are other issues to contend with as well.

Leadership itself is something that is now being called into question. As I noted earlier in this essay, I have seen strong tendencies in many synagogues and churches to establish more decentralized leadership infrastructures, partly to make them feel less like institutions. As a member of the clergy, I am ambivalent about this trend. Ministers, priests, and rabbis are highly educated and trained to be the authoritative voices and transmitters of their religions, yet we live in an era in which authority is perpetually challenged. If the ordained cleric doesn't have the final say on spiritual matters for his or her spiritual community, then who does? Should our post-9/11 congregations make decisions by majority rule, or by some other mechanism?

In my view and based on my experience, a healthy congregation or community requires an active and dynamic partnership between its clergy and lay leaders. In some areas, the trained (and called!) religious "professional" must have the final word; in others (fiscal matters, for instance), where the clergyperson has no serious training, the decisions must be made by those who do. Since congregations are human constructions, power struggles are inevitable. Yet if the lines of responsibility, as well as *authority*, are made sharp and clear, many of the problems I have witnessed can be mitigated.

The trick is to be authoritative without becoming authoritarian.

If trust, humility, and love—the tripartite elements of any successful human relationship—do not inhere in the leadership body and core values of a religious institution, it will be doomed to dysfunction or disintegration. Interdependence, not internecine feuds, must serve as the cornerstone and fuel of today's faith community.

In this post-9/11 context, nothing will ever be the same—or, as the Greek philosopher Heraclitus observed thousands of years ago, nothing ever is. That ought not be a cause for us to despair. Rather, it represents an opportunity as well as a challenge. As religious leaders for this new millennium, our task is to provide authentic spiritual anchors that will make the members of our many and varied faith communities feel safe and secure, while simultaneously offering them exciting, eclectic, and innovative approaches to living religious lives that will speak to them in a language that they will find accessible, enriching, and, in the end, transformational. We owe them no less.

What does our biblical heritage have to say about this issue, namely, responding creatively (and with credibility) to unforeseen challenges? Quite a bit, it turns out. To grasp its teachings, however, we need to move beyond playing the numbers game. Yes, the number of Jews and Christians affiliating with or attending mainstream synagogues and churches has declined. Yes, we need to rethink and re-vision what it means to be religious in this new world. But we must act out of courage, not fear.

Size doesn't matter. What matters is commitment and creativity.

As far back as the Bible, in the book of 1 Samuel (chapter 17), the young and diminutive David, long before he became a great king, defeated the Philistine adversary and giant, Goliath, on an open battlefield in the valley of Elah. David emerged unbowed and victorious because he used focus, faith, and fierce determination. While his fellow Israelites cringed in terror on the sidelines in the face of seemingly overwhelming odds and obstacles, David stepped up to the challenge. We all know the story. But the true message is this: The sling and stone that cracked the giant's skull should be viewed, through the modern lens, as symbolic extensions of David's will and imagination.

He was the real deal—not the restrained and serene version sculpted by Michelangelo many centuries later that stands, almost complacently, in Florence. The genuine David was characterized by a fiery tenacity, by guts, and by a total refusal to submit to conventional tactics. He is a metaphor for the kind of religion we need now.

It is, paradoxically, as traditional a model as it is cutting edge.

Our preoccupation with statistics and membership rolls is rooted in fear, self-doubt, and jealousy. These are all deeply corrosive forces to us as religious leaders, and they should be jettisoned from our minds and hearts as soon as possible. Brash, bold, and sometimes irreverent strategies for reimagining our faith traditions, our spiritual identities, and our concepts of community should be our current focus. Interestingly, that was also the focus of some of our greatest and most effective biblical heroes. And that is what will lead to the survival and vitality of pluralistic religion in America today.

Let me return to my own religion for a moment. During the Passover Seder, we read a famous verse from the Torah that has a lot to teach us about vision and the path to communal growth: "My father was a wandering Aramean. He went down to Egypt, few in number, and sojourned there. And there he became a great nation" (Deut. 26:5, my translation). The patriarch Jacob—also known as Israel and a symbol of the Jewish people as a whole—recounts the exodus narrative with a mixture of humility and pride. He is the son of a nomad, a member of a clan. Yet he is also a link in a sacred chain that stretches across generations, an eternal, unbreakable chain that transcends time and space.

Start small, think big. Quality, not quantity, must be our goal as religious leaders.

Our tiny ancestral band of nomadic tribes became a mighty nation and brought monotheism to the world—but only after years of struggle and sacrifice. Christianity, our sister religion, emerged later and evolved in its own unique ways. Which leaves us where we stand today, struggling to figure out, sometimes collectively and sometimes apart, what our next pathways as religions, and religious communities, might be.

No Egypt can destroy a faithful people's ferocious will to live.

No culture can constrain creative minds determined to break free.

CHAPTER 8

Living the Story

~

DIANA BUTLER BASS

For three years, I researched vital mainline Protestant congregations. Armed with a grant from the Lilly Endowment, I studied fifty churches to determine if there existed a
common pattern of spiritual vibrancy and shared practices that
strengthened communal life. Sifting through thousands of pages of data, my team pieced together both an overall pattern and
leading practices in the study group, thus developing a picture
of religious change, emerging vitality, and potential futures for
mainline Protestantism.[1]

As a result of this project, many clergy groups have invited
me to share my findings; I estimate that I have now addressed
nearly 20,000 clergy and lay leaders across the United States
(with a good number of Canadians in the mix). From place to
place, people asked a variety of questions, engaging the research
in productive ways. At every event, however, someone raised
questions of leadership: "What did you observe about leadership? What kind of leadership nurtures the kind of vitality you
found? What are the characteristics of the leaders in these congregations?" I quickly realized that in most cases people were
asking me how they could lead their congregations into a richer life in God. And, sadly, they felt frustrated in their own at-
tempts to be good leaders. The questions seemed to come from

their own spiritual hunger, a nagging sense of failure as congregational leaders, or anxiety about their leadership performance.

My research team did not directly study leadership in vital congregations—we hoped to make that the topic of a later grant. Early on, I actually tried to avoid questions of leadership, feeling vaguely inadequate to address the topic and having no specific data to share. I worry that leadership is difficult to discuss and prone to "magic bullet" solutions of quick-fix gurus. The questions kept coming, however, and although I had no hard data, I realized that I had observed good leadership in the participating congregations. In *The Practicing Congregation*, the first book published about the project, I identified an emerging style of "narrative leadership" for congregational renewal.[2]

Narrative leadership is a deceptively simple principle: know your story and live it. Some people know stories and tell them well but live without intentional connection to those stories; others simply experience quotidian life with no reflection on larger stories of meaning. In vital mainline churches, leaders knew their stories and lived them—thus turning the power of narrative into a source of and resource for change.

While *The Practicing Congregation* was primarily theoretical, this essay develops narrative leadership by discerning four pathways of practice in the study churches. These pathways serve as entry points for those unfamiliar with this vision of leadership and signposts to keep current practitioners moving ahead. They include: (1) story shapes leadership; (2) leaders shape stories; (3) narrative leadership is character and context driven; and (4) leadership is based in charisma, not celebrity.

Pathway 1: Story Shapes Leadership

The stories about American religion shape our expectations of leadership. For example, "the *Titanic*" story line dominates how we talk about mainline Protestantism. We think of mainline Protestant denominations as a doomed ocean liner, the ship has hit an iceberg (political conflict, numerical decline, or some other crisis) and is sinking. Denominational officials are accused of "rearranging deck chairs on the *Titanic*." People regularly remark, "We're going down," or "We can't turn this ship around." Once, I heard an Episcopalian refer to her priest as "the chaplain on the *Titanic*."

If we think of churches as the *Titanic*, that has serious implications for leadership—our bishops, conference ministers, pastors, and priests are required to rescue us. Throw people in lifeboats. Fix the big hole in the ship. Save whoever—and whatever—can be saved. From this perspective, leadership is an emergency rescue operation, heroic but hopeless. We all know the end of the story. The ship will sink. The best our leaders can do is to save a few—and maybe themselves. No wonder so many pastors are anxious and depressed. Who wants to lead in this scenario?

But what if the *Titanic* is not the story? A better story—and perhaps more accurate in current circumstances—may be that of the *Mayflower*. In this story, a boat of Pilgrims finds itself in uncharted seas, blown off course by a storm and heading to an unnamed country. Like the *Titanic* story, there is a sense of urgency, confusion, and fear. But the ship is intact as it sails off course from the intended colony of Virginia. Here, leaders are not trying to patch the hull or load lifeboats. They are not praying for a miracle. Instead, they look for land. They keep calm while providing focus, vision, and direction, while they navigate the choppy—if unfamiliar—seas of the north Atlantic. Once they do reach land, leaders envision a way to structure the new community and take part in building a new life.

In the *Titanic* story, leaders lead while the ship is sinking. In the *Mayflower* story, leadership stabilizes a Pilgrim community in choppy seas as they head for an unknown world. Leadership in a crisis? Or leadership as an adventure? How a leader leads and the expectations a community has about leadership depends on the stories we tell ourselves.

Pathway 2: Leaders Shape Stories

Closely related to this is the capacity of leaders to shape stories. These days, one of the primary capacities of good leadership is to enable people to understand change, interpret chaos, and make sense of a seemingly meaningless world. There are a variety of ways for leaders to make meaning—some religions practice this sort of leadership through creedal conformity, dictates, demands, or intellectual certainty. But another route to meaning-making is through storytelling.

Throughout my research on vital mainline churches, both clergy and congregational leaders were storytellers. They knew their own faith stories, they knew the stories of their congregations, they knew their tradition's stories, and they knew the larger Christian and biblical stories. They exhibited ease and comfort in sharing these stories and invited others into a variety of stories in natural and authentic ways. In the process, they opened paths for other people to learn and tell stories of faith. And they ably moved between personal, congregational, and biblical stories to create worlds of spiritual and theological meaning. They intuited the power of story to rearrange people's lives—using story in much the same way Jesus did—and to open windows to spiritual realities and alternative paths that sometimes escape life's more mundane interpretations.

And, of course, storytelling leaders have the ability to change the story in which they exercise leadership! Scripts can be rewritten. A good leader will be able to move a congregation away from deadening and fear-filled stories, like that of the *Titanic*, toward life-giving possibilities of faithful adventure.

Pathway 3: Leadership Is
Character and Context Driven

Every pastoral leader I met—and every lay leader I interviewed—acted as a uniquely formed "character" in his or her story. Each person had a specific faith journey, each particular gifts for leadership, each a distinctive vision of God's reign, and each a set of practices that shaped ministry. In no circumstance did any person resemble a clone of another—they allowed their personhood to shape their leadership practices. They understood that leadership emerged from the crucible of personal health and healthy relationships—it was not guaranteed on the basis of a role they held or an external authority structure. The more individuals leaned into their own strengths, the more they trusted who God made them to be, the more richly they discovered their own abilities as leaders.

Although they demonstrated no single set of characteristics, there were some leadership commonalities across the study. They did not depend on external definitions of leadership, but they were familiar with a variety of leadership theories and tools. Nearly all the clergy had read Ron Heifetz's book *Leadership without Easy Answers* and practiced adaptive leadership in concert with appropriate use of technical skills.[3] They were good pastors and preachers; they knew their strengths and weaknesses; they exercised humor and humility. And they realized their own ministry was strengthened in relation to the whole of the congregation (this was true for lay leaders as well).

Thus, uniqueness existed within the context of community. Good character-driven leadership did not rise above or control the congregation on the basis of personality or charisma. Instead, religious leadership functioned best in a connected network of relationships; characters worked in concert with each other deepening and developing the larger plotlines of the congregation. In developing connection, there needed to be some sort of "match" or "fit," some sort of almost indefinable meshing, between the personhood of the leader and the congregation context. In the language of story, characters need to live reflexively with the setting.

Many of the pastors in my project had learned this through experience. A good number of them had struggled in earlier placements or calls—they never connected because the settings were wrong for their own character. But when the clergyperson found his or her way to the "right" congregation, then their own practice of leadership soared. Excellent pastoral leadership is, indeed, individual and unique, but it is not separate or singular; it is deeply embedded in the context of community. And it must be developed there in healthy, emotionally mature, and spiritually wise ways.

Pathway 4: Leadership Is Based in Charisma, Not Celebrity

When I am quizzed about the pastors in my project, other clergy frequently ask if these leaders were particularly charismatic and if congregational renewal depended upon a strong personality. Most of the time, this question is posed in a critical manner—as if there is something inappropriate or dangerous about charismatic leadership. Indeed, many of the clergy who participated in the study were interesting and talented people, with varying levels of personal charisma. Their charisma was distinct from religious celebrity. Rather, charisma—giftedness in the biblical sense—emerged from integrity through practicing what they preached.

Many congregants praised their clergy (or other spiritual leaders in their churches) as "real" or "authentic." They related a number of characteristics with authenticity, including the ability to relate to a wide variety of people, being open, accessible, funny, and "very human." However, along with such down-to-earth qualities, congregants further extolled spiritual leaders who embodied their theological beliefs through identifiable Christian practices. Congregations wanted ministers who practiced hospitality, stayed centered in prayer, ordered their economic lives through stewardship and generosity, and testified to God's transforming grace in their own experience. Thus, a mixture of personable "just like us" qualities and the ability to model practical spirituality seemed optimal for leaders.

Clergy and other spiritual leaders may find this difficult, but I thought these expectations surprisingly humane. Leaders need to be serious faith practitioners, people who "walk the talk" and live out the things they hope will change the lives of others. However, the congregations in my project did not want a pastor's devotion to separate the minister and people; they did not appear to want super-saints as leaders. They wanted spiritually mature, very human leaders—the same balance they hoped to achieve in their own lives.

Leaders in the study cultivated a life of practice. But they knew that not every person is called to every Christian practice—some people are more gifted or skilled at certain ones. Thus, the ministers prayed, but they recognized that others might be more mature in the practice of prayer and willingly became learners in relation to able practitioners. They knew when to lead in practice, and they equally knew when to learn from the wisdom of other people in the congregation. Religious leaders need to practice what they preach, but they need not be perfect in their practice. Practicing what one preaches does not imply perfection. Rather, it means creating a certain level of congruence between proclaiming faith and demonstrating it in one's life.

One of the most dramatic cultural shifts of the last thirty years is in the role storytelling plays in our lives; story has become a primary path to meaning-making. Sociologist Anthony

Giddens claims that our identity is found "in the on-going story about the self" and further asserts that "each of us not only 'has' but lives a biography."[4] Moral philosopher Charles Taylor says that we understand life as an "unfolding story" in which "we grasp our lives as narrative."[5] Put simply, we become ourselves as we tell our stories. We cannot know ourselves apart from our stories—stories in which we are both author and actor. When these philosophical principles are expanded beyond the individual to congregation, the power of narrative leadership is easily grasped and naturally enacted.[6] To lead is to create story and to act in concert with the tale.

Notes

1. For more on the this project and its findings, see Diana Butler Bass, *The Practicing Congregation: Imagining a New Old Church* (Herndon, VA: Alban Institute, 2004); Diana Butler Bass and Joseph Stewart-Sicking, *From Nomads to Pilgrims: Stories from Practicing Congregations* (Herndon, VA: Alban Institute, 2006); and Diana Butler Bass, *Christianity for the Rest of Us: How the Neighborhood Church Is Transforming the Faith* (San Francisco: HarperSanFrancisco, 2006). See also www.dianabutlerbass.com.

2. Bass, *The Practicing Congregation*, 91–102.

3. Ronald A. Heifetz, *Leadership Without Easy Answers* (Cambridge, MA: The Belknap Press of Harvard University, 1994).

4. Anthony Giddens, *Modernity and Self-Identity* (Stanford, CA: Stanford University Press, 1991), 54.

5. Charles Taylor, *Sources of the Self* (Cambridge, MA: Harvard University Press, 1989), 47.

6. For the transformative power of story in congregations, see Lillian Daniel, *Tell It Like It Is: Reclaiming the Practice of Testimony* (Herndon, VA: Alban Institute, 2006).

Contributors

~

Diana Butler Bass is an author, speaker, and independent scholar specializing in American religion and culture. She holds a Ph.D. in religious studies from Duke University and is the author of seven books, including *A People's History of Christianity: The Other Side of the Story*, *Christianity for the Rest of Us: How the Neighborhood Church Is Transforming the Faith*, and *The Practicing Congregation: Imagining a New Old Church*. From 2002 to 2006, she was the project director of a national Lilly Endowment-funded study of mainline Protestant vitality.

Niles Elliot Goldstein is Rabbi Emeritus of The New Shul in Manhattan and the award-winning author or editor of nine books, most recently *The Challenge of the Soul: A Guide for the Spiritual Warrior*. His book *Gonzo Judaism* was honored by *Publishers Weekly* and *Kirkus Reviews* as one of the best religion/spirituality books of 2007.

Larry A. Golemon is an ordained Presbyterian minister and a consultant and researcher in theological education. He co-authored *Educating Clergy: Teaching Practices and Pastoral Imagination*, the Carnegie Foundation study of seminaries, and recently directed the Narrative Leadership project for the Alban Institute and the Ecumenical Project at Virginia Theological Seminary.

Carol Johnston was ordained in the Presbyterian Church (USA) thirty years ago and is associate professor of theology and culture at Christian Theological Seminary in Indianapolis. She is working on a book on faith and generosity.

Mike Mather is the pastor of Broadway United Methodist Church in Indianapolis. He has served urban churches in the state of Indiana for more than twenty-four years. He is the author of *Sharing Stories, Shaping Community* in the series Vital Ministry in the Small Membership Church.

G. Lee Ramsey Jr., an ordained United Methodist minister, is the Marlon and Sheila Foster Professor of Pastoral Theology and Homiletics at Memphis Theological Seminary. Ramsey writes film and fiction reviews for explorefaith. org and is the author of *Preachers and Misfits, Prophets and Thieves: The Minister in Southern Fiction.*

Tim Shapiro is president of the Indianapolis Center for Congregations, a supporting organization of the Alban Institute funded by the Lilly Endowment. A minister in the Presbyterian Church (USA), he has served in pastoral ministry for almost twenty years. He has served congregations in Ohio and Indiana.

N. Graham Standish, PhD, MSW, is pastor of Calvin Presbyterian Church in Zelienople, Pennsylvania. He is author of five books, including *Humble Leadership* and *Becoming the Blessed Church*, both Alban books. In addition, he is a spiritual director, therapist, retreat leader and teacher, and an adjunct professor at Pittsburgh Theological Seminary, focusing in the areas of spirituality and congregational leadership.